Time Well Spent

FAMILY HIKING
IN THE SMOKIES

We dedicate this book to our children who have helped us see the Smokies in new ways.

We're grateful for the hard work, support and patience of Elizabeth, Janice and Lin.

Trails Illustrated has two maps of Great Smoky Mountains National Park available. The paper recreation map is keyed to this book. To order maps write Trails Illustrated at P.O. Box 3610 Evergreen, Colorado or call 1-800-962-1643

Published by
Panther Press
P.O. Box 636
Seymour, Tennessee 37865

Acknowledgements

Photography Credits: Cover photograph of Andrews Bald by Janice Maynard

Back cover photograph by Ernie Tracy of Tracy Photography

Pages 7, 24, 36, 81 & 87 Hal Hubbs; page 94 Elizabeth Hubbs; pages 11, 26, 52 & 61 David Morris; page 42 Charles Maynard and page 48 Janice Maynard

Maps by Charles Maynard

Cover & book design by Rusk Design, 115 Givens Street, Fountain Inn, SC 29644

We are grateful for the assistance of the National Park Service, Lynn Alexander, Nancy Best, Fred Hopkins, Cathy Maggard, Bob and Joyce Rusk, Ernie Tracy and Teresa Wright.

 Printed on recycled paper

Time Well Spent
FAMILY HIKING
IN THE SMOKIES

Hal Hubbs, Charles Maynard & David Morris

Panther Press SEYMOUR TENNESSEE

THIRD EDITION

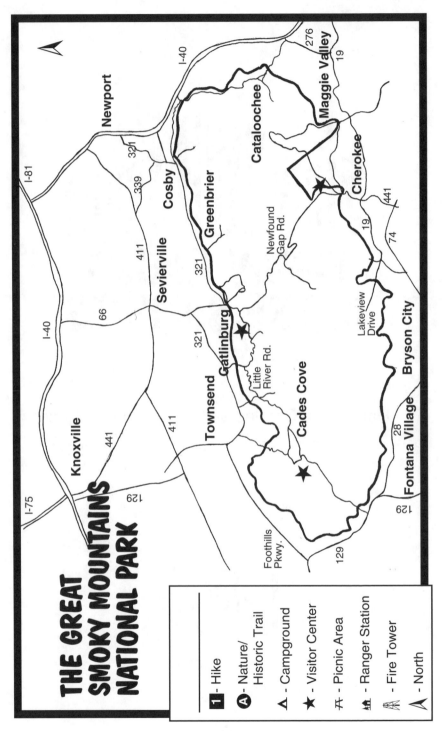

THE GREAT SMOKY MOUNTAINS NATIONAL PARK

Legend:
- **1** - Hike
- **Ⓐ** - Nature/ Historic Trail
- **⛺** - Campground
- **★** - Visitor Center
- **🌲** - Picnic Area
- **🏠** - Ranger Station
- **🗼** - Fire Tower
- **↑** - North

Knoxville, Newport, Sevierville, Cosby, Greenbrier, Cataloochee, Maggie Valley, Cherokee, Gatlinburg, Townsend, Cades Cove, Bryson City, Fontana Village

I-75, I-81, I-40, I-40, 441, 129, 411, 66, 339, 321, 321, 321, 411, 321, Little River Rd., Newfound Gap Rd., Foothills Pkwy., Lakeview Drive, 28, 129, 129, 19, 276, 19, 441, 74

TABLE OF CONTENTS

Hiking in the mountains is fun but potentially dangerous. Please use every precaution and good sense when visiting the park. Observe all posted warnings and park regulations. The authors and publisher are not responsible for injury, loss or damage incurred from the use of this guide.

TIPS FOR FAMILY HIKING

The Great Smoky Mountains National Park offers many opportunities for family recreation. One enjoyable way to experience the park is to hike some of its 800+ miles of trails. As precious as family leisure time is, it shouldn't be wasted. This book suggests many ways to enjoy the mountains and your family in the limited time available.

Family hiking doesn't have to be a frustrating struggle, but it does involve more than just walking a mountain trail. The key to enjoyment is planning ahead.

First, pick a hike that is suited to your child's abilities. We've rated hikes according to age ranges. As wonderful as some hikes may be, your preschooler may not be able to make them. The more difficult hikes allow teens to feel a sense of accomplishment. If your child hikes a lot she may be up to more difficult walks; an easier introduction would be better for a child who has never been on a hike.

Allow plenty of time. Our time estimates are generous. Much of the enjoyment of the hike should be the actual walk rather than the destination. Your child will remember the experience of being with you longer than the scenery he sees. Relax and walk at your child's pace.

Since children's eyes are closer to the ground, they will see things that you might miss. Be prepared to saunter or you'll seem a relentless trail boss driving the herd onward. Such an attitude may mean you don't go as far, but the hike with the family is the objective, not the destination.

The old scout motto, "Be Prepared," is a good one for family hiking. Try to think ahead to a child's needs for the entire time on the trail. We always walk with plenty of water and toilet paper (although it seems that if you use less of the former you can use less of the latter). One canteen for every two people is our best guess. A first aid kit and rain gear are important. Even on the clearest summer mornings, an afternoon thundershower can drench you. It's nice to have an extra set of clothing in the car.

Wear proper clothing. Remember that mountain temperatures are cooler. Keep a jacket in the car in ALL seasons. Allow for wind and rain when choosing what to wear. We often travel with two pairs of shoes and socks, an old pair that can get wet and dirty and a good pair that's left in the car. Always wear tennis shoes or boots, never sandals or flip-flops. Also, loose-fitting, play clothes are usually more comfortable for walking. It's difficult to fully enjoy a hike if keeping clothes clean is a priority.

In being prepared, don't over-burden yourself. Allow even the youngest to carry some portion of the load. Most children are eager to carry a small pack or fanny pack with part of lunch, the first aid kit or binoculars. Be prepared, but don't carry the kitchen sink.

Some other things we take are: snacks, small flashlight, magnifying glass, peppermints (or chewing gum), binoculars, flower book, water, rain gear, sun screen, matches, camera, extra film, and a whistle for each child.

First Aid Kit

•Adhesive Strip Bandages	•Antiseptic Cream
•Sterile Gauze Pads	•Moleskin
•Adhesive Tape	•Children's & Adult Pain Reliever
•Alcohol Pads	•Knife with Scissors & Tweezers
•"Space" Blanket for Emergency Warmth	

We carry plenty of water because water along the trail is unsafe to drink. Put an open canteen almost full with water into the freezer the night before a summer hike. The solid ice will slowly melt the next day while walking. This will provide cool water along the way. All mountain water must be boiled or chemically treated to be safe. Even the most remote mountain areas carry a risk. We usually carry water purification tablets for emergencies.

Safety first! A few rules are helpful to keep a hike fun and safe. Stay on the trail! This is important for children to understand. It's easy to get lost in a laurel thicket or in dense undergrowth; plus, the forest can be damaged by off trail walking. Let each child have a whistle which is to be used only in emergencies. (Practice blowing these before you get on the trail.)

In case of bathroom emergencies, a few rules are to be followed. Stay away from water sources. Get off the trail at least 100 feet and dig a hole 6 inches deep. Cover the hole when finished.

It's fun to hold hands, and with younger children essential, but be mindful of over-holding. Walking with hand over head (even if it is supported) for fifteen or twenty minutes can be most uncomfortable. (Try it yourself.) Some trails allow a family to spread out. Keep your children in sight but allow them to go ahead or linger behind.

Pay attention to the signals your child gives you. Stop for frequent breaks to rest, play, dawdle, look, and splash. If your child becomes irritable and doesn't want to continue try distracting them with a game. Talk **with** your child, instead of **to** your child. When all else fails, turn around. It is better to have a pleasant experience on a short walk than a miserable one on a longer trail. The memory will be of time with you in the mountains rather than that time my parents yelled at me on the trail.

Use all the senses. Explore smells, textures, and tastes. Children are apt to learn more through their senses than through the passing on of information. They're also more likely to remember the sensory experiences. The forest has many sounds. Help your children listen quietly for a few minutes every now and then. It's too much to expect them to be quiet for long periods. Sometimes we play listening games. "How many different sounds can you hear?" "How many different birds can you hear?" "How many sounds does a waterfall make?" Try

Suggested Items for Safe Family Hiking

- Plenty of Water
- Snacks, Chewing Gum or Peppermints
- Appropriate Footwear - Such as Athletic Shoes or Boots not sandals or flip flops.
- Toilet Paper or Tissues
- Sunscreen
- Small First Aid Kit
- Rain Gear
- Whistle for Each Child
- Flashlight
- Waterproof Matches
- Water-purification Tablets
- Extra Clothing
- Extras to Add Interest - Wildflower and Bird Books, Magnifying Glass, Binoculars, and Camera with Extra Film
- Garbage Bags - Can be used for trash, waterproof seat, rain gear or pack cover

a five minute silent walk to see what wildlife may be encountered. This can change the routine and may yield some interesting results.

Point out interesting things but be slow to explain. Allow your child to draw their own conclusions. Assist with questions and observations. "What do you think made these rocks smooth?" "How do you think these boulders got here?" "What would it have been like to live in this cabin?" Let those who can, read brochures and booklets to the whole family. In this way, the child can be the teacher instead of the student.

Creek play is a fun, refreshing way to end a hike. Throwing rocks and sticks into creeks is fun when barefoot and in the water. Be careful of slick rocks and strong current. The water is usually very cold, but children don't seem to mind it as much as adults. Cold water on tired feet feels great.

An ice cold drink in a cooler at the car is a wonderful treat! A light snack is also nice to have waiting. These ease the trip back to the motel or home.

The hikes in this book are arranged geographically by areas. The mileages are approximations as are the park signs. An index in the back provides an easy way to identify features of the individual hikes. These are our favorites which we hope you enjoy.

We've included interesting stories, natural features and points of interest. Our goal is for families to enjoy the Great Smoky Mountains National Park together. The experience of being with your children can be a most enjoyable one with patience and a little planning. Truly, Time Well Spent!

THE GREAT SMOKY MOUNTAINS NATIONAL PARK

The Great Smoky Mountains National Park is the most visited national park in the United States, with over 10 million visits each year. Biological diversity is one of the trademarks which draws people from all over the world to this mountain sanctuary. With species numbering over 1,500 flowering plants, 50 ferns, and 130 trees, the park is a botanical wonder. Also finding a home in the area are over 70 mammal, 35 reptile, 35 amphibian, 230 bird, and 45 fish species. Several species of animals are being reintroduced. The red wolf, peregrine falcon, otter, and brook trout, which were once natives, are finding a home here again. A small part of the spruce-fir forest endangered by a tiny aphid is being treated to preserve the trees. These efforts are among many that are ongoing in the park.

The story of the Great Smoky Mountains begins over 230 million years ago when movements in the earth's crust thrust up mountains. Over millions of years, wind and rain wore the mighty mountains down. Too far south for the glacial forces of the ice age, the Smokies became a haven for northern flora and fauna such as spruce-fir trees.

Native Americans arrived only several thousand years ago. The Cherokee were the last native Americans to live and hunt in the Smokies. White settlers immigrated to the area in the late 1700s and early 1800s pressuring the Cherokee to move out. The forcible removal of the Cherokee became known as the Trail of Tears. One in four Cherokee died on the trail to Oklahoma during this dark time in the history of the region. To avoid the removal, some Cherokee found refuge in the Smokies where their descendants remain.

White settlers moved into the valleys and coves to farm and herd. In the late 1800s and early 1900s, logging and mining came to the Smoky Mountains. Many worked as loggers, miners, railroaders, and suppliers. In the 1920s, concern for preserving the area arose. The Appalachian Trail was constructed and the National Park Service was started. Although many people worked tirelessly to establish a national park, many families' homes were sacrificed for the park to come into being.

The Great Smoky Mountains National Park is an international biosphere which attempts to preserve geological, biological, and botanical diversity as well as human history. Many people never get out of their car as they zip along the highways. However, the Park Service provides excellent opportunities to experience the Great Smoky Mountains in a more complete way. The three visitor centers are good places to start. Each offers a theme which displays a different aspect of the Smokies. At Sugarlands near Gatlinburg, a museum and movie introduce the visitor to the diversity of plant and animal life. The life of the early settler can be better understood with a visit to Oconaluftee near Cherokee. The Cades Cove Center offers a closer look at a mill and life on a mountain cove farm with many interpretive programs.

At each of the visitor centers is a resource center operated by the Great Smoky Mountains Natural History Association. Most of the books on the resource list in the back of this book can be bought along with other materials such as videos, posters, maps, and tapes. A valuable resource at the visitor centers is the park newspaper, Smokies Guide. This lists the many programs in the park, including ranger-led activities, which are free of charge. Also, brochures about various aspects of the park are available for a small charge.

Ten campgrounds provide beautiful settings for overnight stays within the park. A nominal fee is paid at the entrance to the campground before setting up camp. Some campgrounds are closed in the winter. Popular sites are difficult to get in the summer. Also, horseback riding is available in the park through authorized concessions. Check at a visitor center for more information.

The picnic areas in the park provide clean restroom facilities, picnic tables and fire grates at scenic spots. Most are closed in the winter but are wonderful places to enjoy a meal in the other seasons. Ask a ranger for a Junior Ranger booklet. The Junior Ranger program is open to children ages 8-12. The activities include picking up a bag of litter, attending ranger-led walks or talks, walking on a self-guided trail, and doing the activities in the booklet. A Junior Ranger badge can be earned when the requirements are completed.

The self-guided nature and auto trails are other ways to get a closer look at the wonders called the Smoky Mountains. Try one of the Quiet Walkways which are located throughout the park and are less than half a mile long. You'll see and enjoy more when you drive slowly and get out of the car often.

The Spring Wildflower Pilgrimage is held every year for three days on the third weekend in April. Hikes, programs, motorcades and children's activities are offered each spring. Write or ask the national park for more information. Also, every year on the fourth Saturday in June, there is a day of storytelling in Cades Cove. Local storytellers relate tales of the mountains at the Cable Mill area. Several other special events are held at Oconaluftee, Cades Cove and Sugarlands. Information is available in the park's newspaper, Smokies Guide, or at the visitor centers.

It's difficult to have time for a vacation or a day off. When that time does become available, it's best to spend it wisely. We hope that families will have a good experience in the Great Smoky Mountains National Park - will have Time Well Spent.

A Word About Wildlife And Plants

Aside from the beautiful vistas, the plants and wildlife found in the Great Smoky Mountains National Park make it unique. In fact, many people visit only to see wildflowers in bloom or to catch a glimpse of a bear. Animals and plants in any ecosystem are in a delicate balance; with millions visiting the Smokies each year, a disregard for this fact could spell disaster.

Following are some tips to insure the beauty of the Smoky Mountains (whatever you perceive it to be) will be around for our children and grandchildren to enjoy.

•Always stay on maintained trails; leaving the trail may damage young plants or disrupt nesting animals.

•Enjoy the beauty of wildflowers by lingering and taking pictures, never pick or damage plants in any way; this is a federal offense.

•Never approach any wildlife, not even deer or chipmunks.

•Never entice animals with food, this causes immediate danger to you and long term danger to the animals.

•If you are fortunate enough to see a bear, enjoy it from a distance; if you meet one on a trail, give it plenty of room.

•Never leave food or packs unattended; if a bear approaches during a picnic, quickly gather everything and move away.

•Only two poisonous snakes are found in the Great Smoky Mountains National Park, the rattlesnake and copperhead. Although snake encounters are rare, use caution; again, stay on the trail and keep a watchful eye when crossing logs or brush.

•Report any aggressive animals or dangerous situations to the nearest ranger.

Enjoy hiking, but as always, use common sense.

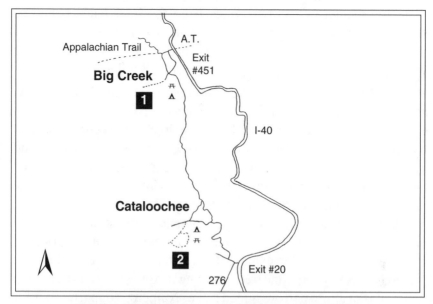

BIG CREEK - CATALOOCHEE

The Big Creek - Cataloochee areas are some of the most scenic in the entire park. Big Creek is popular due to its proximity to the interstate while Cataloochee is an undiscovered treasure found by few. Both can be seen in a day trip or enjoyed for longer periods by staying in the campgrounds at either.

From the Walnut Bottom area to its junction with the Pigeon River, Big Creek drops about 1,200 feet (120 stories), or an average of 200 feet per mile. The change in elevation causes many beautiful cascades and small falls on this large creek. The trail stays close to the creek so its sights and sounds can be fully enjoyed.

The Big Creek Basin was logged by the Crestmont Lumber Company in the early 1900s. Many of the trails follow old logging railroad beds. Evidence of the logging days can be found - steel cables, rails, spikes, and old roadbeds. The forest, mostly hardwoods and spruce-fir, has recovered well from the logging.

To reach Big Creek, take the Waterville Exit on I-40 about 60 miles east of Knoxville or 50 miles west of Asheville. Cross the Pigeon River and turn left at the end of the bridge over which the Appalachian Trail crosses. Follow the road past the Walters Power

Plant to an intersection two miles from the interstate. Continue straight through the intersection up a narrow road to the Ranger Station. The picnic area and campground, which are closed in the winter, are beyond the ranger station about 0.8 miles.

At the eastern end of the Great Smoky Mountains National Park, a remote valley offers tales of the past. As the 1900s began, Cataloochee was the largest settlement in the Smokies with some 200 buildings. The valley was once owned by Colonel Robert Love, a land speculator. As the area around Cataloochee grew, Col. Love granted homesteads to those who agreed to settle and improve the land. Some of the early families were Caldwell, Hannah, Bennett, Noland, Palmer, Franklin, Woody and Barnes. Descendants of these families lived here as late as the 1960s. The name Cataloochee comes from the Cherokee "Gadalutsi" meaning "fringe standing erect." This was probably in reference to the trees growing in rows along the side of the mountains or atop a narrow spined ridge. Numerous opportunities for hiking, picnicking, and sightseeing are available in Cataloochee.

Two routes access Cataloochee. Exit I-40 at U.S. 276 (Exit #20-Maggie Valley in North Carolina). Turn right on Cove Creek Road after the interstate exit. The paved road ends after 1-1/2 miles but resumes after 7-1/2 miles at the park boundary. The 11 miles from the interstate to Cataloochee is a scenic drive.

The other route begins at Big Creek. Exit I-40 at the Waterville Exit. Follow the above directions toward the Big Creek Ranger Station. At the intersection two miles from the interstate, turn left. This road, a well maintained gravel road, leads 16 miles to Cataloochee. Sometimes we use one route going in and another coming out. Either way, Cataloochee is a wonderful treat which shouldn't be missed. The campground is closed and no restrooms are available in the winter.

The cardinal or red bird was called "Daughter of the Sun" by the Cherokee.

1. Midnight Hole & Mouse Creek Falls
- 4 miles roundtrip
- Allow 5 to 6 hours

Elementary children can hike this moderate walk along a beautiful creek to two waterfalls.

How to Get There: Take the Waterville Exit at I-40 about 60 miles east of Knoxville and 50 miles west of Asheville. Cross the Pigeon River and turn left at the end of the bridge over which the Appalachian Trail passes. Follow the road past the Walters Power Plant to an intersection two miles from the interstate. Continue straight through the intersection up a narrow road to the Ranger Station. The picnic area and campground are beyond the Ranger Station about 0.8 miles. These are closed in the winter. Pit toilets are at the parking area near the Ranger Station and at the campground.

Description of Hike: The walk is on the Big Creek Trail which begins near the Big Creek Campground. The trail is a wide road bed which makes it easy to walk side by side. The gain in elevation is slight so there is no strain. The trail which is open to hikers and horses is popular, especially with fisherman.

You look down on Big Creek far below at first. Notice the change in rocks along the trail as you pass over the Greenbrier Fault. The stratified Rich Butt Sandstone gives way to the more solid and fine grained Thunderhead Sandstone. By the time the creek is reached all the rock is Thunderhead Sandstone.

Midnight Hole, which is well named, is 1.4 miles from the campground. A large pool is filled with the clear water of Big Creek. The pool is a dark green in the winter and dark as midnight in the summer. Enormous boulders squeeze Big Creek to a small opening through which two falls of eight feet pour. In wet weather, water spills over the rock that divides the two to form a single falls. At Midnight Hole are remnants of the logging industry which worked this area. Steel cable and rails are in the woods and among the rocks. Midnight Hole is a wonderful place for a picnic, a nice rest or a pretty photo.

Continue on up the trail 0.6 miles beside the roaring Big Creek to Mouse Creek Falls. A hitching rail on the left indicates the place to walk over to view the falls. A bench provides a pleasant place to observe the 50 foot falls. Mouse Creek Falls is a beautiful hour glass cascade at the mouth of Mouse Creek. Several streams twine together to form a wide base of falling water. A small pool at the base slows the water as it crosses an old logging railroad bed.

The return to your car is easy and allows for another opportunity to look at Midnight Hole. This walk is fine in any season. Just remember that in winter the gate is closed on the road to the campground. Thus, 1.6 miles is added to the roundtrip mileage.

2. Caldwell Fork & Boogerman Loop
- 5.6 miles or 7.4 miles roundtrip
- Allow 3 to 5 hours

Elementary and **teens** will find this a pleasant moderate walk through virgin forest. The most difficult segment is from the upper junction of the Caldwell Fork and Boogerman Trails where in 1 mile about 800 feet in elevation is gained.

How To Get There: The trailhead is on the Cataloochee Road approximately 300 yards past the campground. Limited parking is available at the trailhead. Restrooms are in the campground but are closed in the winter.

Description Of The Hike: Begin the walk by crossing Cataloochee Creek on a long footlog. Caldwell Fork empties into Cataloochee Creek to the left of the trailhead. Initially the trail follows Caldwell Fork through a flat area of large pine trees with rhododendron growing along the creek. Enjoy the soft path paved with needles under foot.

Caldwell Fork was named for the families that settled along this beautiful creek. After 0.5 miles, the pine forest gives way to virgin hemlock, the trail begins to climb slightly. After crossing Caldwell Fork on a second footlog, at 0.8 miles, the Boogerman Trail enters from the left. Continue straight along Caldwell Fork enjoying the creek and coolness of the virgin forest. This stretch is easy with lots of flat areas and only short inclines. In spring, wildflowers abound along the creek.

Since this is a multi-use trail, wet weather causes numerous boggy spots. Between the upper and lower connections with the Boogerman Loop, the path crosses Caldwell Fork and its tributaries thirteen times on footlogs. Some are without handrails, so take care. They can be wet and slippery.

The trail leaves the creek to ascend slightly to the upper trailhead of the Boogerman Loop. You can return to the parking area by the same route for an easy hike of 5.6 miles. The Caldwell Fork Trail continues up Caldwell Fork another 3.7 miles to a junction with Rough Fork Trail.

An alternate route back to your car is the Boogerman Loop Trail which leaves Caldwell Fork on the left. Boogerman Loop follows Snake Branch through large hemlock for 0.8 miles. Notice the remains of chimneys and stone fences in this flat area which was once well settled. Carson Messer had a large homestead here. A large tuliptree with a den at the base is at 0.6 miles on the left of the trail.

The trail turns to the left and away from Snake Branch at 0.8 miles. It passes through the remnants of an old rail gate as it ascends a finger of Cataloochee Divide toward Den Ridge. The forest here is mixed hardwoods, poplar, and large chestnut oak. Take your time up this stretch. It's the most difficult part of the hike.

Leaving the ridge crest and skirting the base of Den Ridge, the trail passes among some of the largest trees in the park. Enjoy the giants of the deep virgin forest, linger at stream crossings, and look at the wildflowers. An extremely large tuliptree stands to the right of the trail 1.6 miles from the beginning of the Boogerman Loop. The forest changes to mostly white pine before reaching the edge of a clearing, which was the Robert Palmer place.

The Boogerman Trail gets its name from Robert Palmer. It seems, that Palmer was a very shy child, who when asked his name would hide his face and reply, "I'm the Boogerman" -- thus the nickname. When the valley became too crowded for him, Palmer used hand tools to build a road to this remote area. He never allowed timber to be cut on his land.

The remaining two miles of this trail follows Palmer's handbuilt road back to Caldwell Fork. The forest changes from mixed hardwoods to pine to virgin hemlock. Some excellent views of the mountains to the north and west can be enjoyed from vantage points on the ridge. This section is all downhill and the trailhead is reached at 3.8 miles from the beginning of the Boogerman Loop (6.6 miles including the walk up Caldwell Fork). The parking area is 0.8 miles to the right along the Caldwell Fork Trail that you traveled earlier. This entire walk is 7.4 miles roundtrip.

The Cataloochee area is a wonderful historic spot with beautiful forests and flowers. It is popular but not as heavily used as other areas of the park. Access can sometimes be difficult in the winter.

How Deer Got Antlers

Long ago, deer had no antlers. The buck had a smooth head like the doe. Deer was a swift runner and Rabbit was a great jumper. Many of the animals wanted to know which of the two could go farthest in the same time. The animals decided to have a contest, and a fine set of antlers was fashioned and offered as the prize. On the appointed day, all the animals gathered at the edge of a large thicket.

The race was to go through the thicket to the forest on the other side and then back through the thicket. Before the race began, Rabbit asked if he could go through the thicket to find his way, saying he wasn't familiar with the area. Deer and the animals agreed that this was fair.

However, Rabbit was gone such a long time, he was suspected of deceit because he was known for his trickery. After a little longer when he still wasn't back, a messenger was sent to find him. The messenger spyed Rabbit in the middle of the thicket clearing a path. The messenger quietly left and told the other animals. When Rabbit returned, the animals accused him of cheating, which he denied. All the animals went into the thicket where they found the cleared road. It was agreed that no trickster deserved the antler prize and so it was awarded to Deer. To this day, deer wear antlers and rabbits gnaw on brush.

A Cherokee Legend

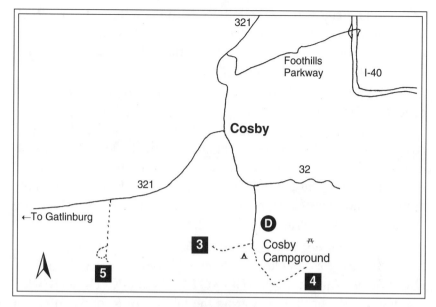

COSBY

Cosby is easily accessible. From Gatlinburg it is 19 miles east on Highway 321, and from I-40 it is 8 miles west on the Foothills Parkway. The Cosby Campground road begins 1.5 miles from the intersection of Highway 321 with Highway 32. After turning off of Highway 32, it is 2 more miles to the Cosby Campground and Picnic Area, where restrooms are found. However, in the winter when the picnic area and campground are closed, a pit toilet is available.

3. Hen Wallow Falls
- 4.2 miles roundtrip
- Allow 2 to 2-1/2 hours

Preschool and **Elementary** children will enjoy this easy to moderate hike which rises 600 feet in 2 miles. This hike offers a creek, waterfall, and colorful fall leaves.

How To Get There: The trailhead is below the Cosby Campground Picnic Area.

Description Of Hike: The first part of the hike is on a slightly rocky roadbed which goes 0.2 miles until a feeder trail from the Cosby

Campground enters from the left. Stay to the right and cross Rock Creek on a footlog. The next 1/2 mile winds through a hardwood forest which gives way to hemlock and rhododendron. A log bench provides an opportunity to rest or play.

At 1.1 miles a stone footbridge crosses Crying Creek to the Gabes Mountain Trail, an old road bed. Crying Creek is so named because a man mistakenly shot his brother while the two were on a bear hunt. After 30 yards follow Gabes Mountain Trail to the left. This stretch is a typical mountain trail with loose rocks and plenty of exposed roots; so, watch your toes and pick up your feet! The trail meanders around the northeastern slopes of Gabes Mountain for one mile before coming to the Hen Wallow Falls trail.

The 700 foot side trail descends to the 95 foot high falls. This part can be tricky for smaller children; so, hold onto hands tightly. **Observe the Warning Signs! <u>DO NOT CLIMB ON THE ROCKS!!</u>** The view to the north (away from the falls) is of Round and Green Mountains. Cosby can be seen in the distance. This is a very enjoyable hike anytime of the year. It's cool in the summer and colorful in the fall. On a visit to Hen Wallow Falls in September, salamanders can be seen all over the rocks beside the falls. Follow the same route back to the campground. This trail is a nice complement to the Cosby Nature Trail which begins at the amphitheater.

4. Mount Cammerer
- 10.4 miles roundtrip
- Allow 6-7 hours

Teens will find this strenuous hike to a mountain peak very challenging. 2,575 feet in altitude is gained in less than 5 miles. This hike offers fine views, spring flowers, colorful fall leaves, and a fire tower.

How To Get There: The trailhead is above the group campsite in the Cosby Campground. Park in the lot provided for hikers below the amphitheater.

Description Of The Hike: Walk on the paved road past the amphitheater through the group camp to a graveled pathway. The trail sign points to the Low Gap and Mt. Cammerer Trails. The gravel jeep road goes past the campground water tower. Opposite the tower in the woods are some old stone walls from houses that were part of a settlement. The jeep road ends at the footlog on Cosby Creek. Before the creek are more stone walls.

The trail gradually ascends through hemlock and rhododendron as it follows Cosby Creek. The creek is inviting on hot summer days but is calming in any season. Two switchbacks move the trail away from the creek through a boulder field. A little branch flows through a drain tile. A rhododendron thicket signals a steeper climb to Low Gap. Beyond the rhododendron is a large tree which is ringed with the methodical work of a yellow-bellied sapsucker in its search for food. The yellow-bellied sapsucker spirals its way up a tree, nearly covering the entire trunk with small holes.

Look for quartz among the rocks of the trail. Patches of mountain laurel, galax, and ferns dot the higher elevations. Carefully cross a small branch and rest by its waters, because the next part is the steepest yet as the trail climbs to Low Gap through hardwoods. At Low Gap the trail meets the Appalachian Trail. Before turning northeast (left) along the Appalachian Trail, enjoy a respite at the gap. There is oak, silverbell, and sweet birch. Sweet birch has black bark with long, pale horizontal lenticels on young trunks and sooty black plates on old trees. When the bark of the twigs is peeled off it tastes and smells of wintergreen.

Continue on the Appalachian Trail to the northeast going through mountain laurel, rhododendron, and galax. A beech and yellow birch grove is along the way. Yellow birch was used by the settlers to make clothespins, toothpicks, and light furniture. The last mile on the A.T. is on a ridge top through rhododendron. At a trail junction is a stand of yellow birch; the A.T. goes to the right while the Mt. Cammerer Trail goes to the left.

The next 0.6 miles is on a ridgeback through spruce, hemlock, rhododendron, mountain laurel, and galax. Before the top, the trail descends to a small gap with a hitching rail. Climb through the rhododendron to the bare, quartz-streaked sandstone rocks of the peak of Mt. Cammerer. The octagonal fire tower was constructed in the 1930s of stone and wood. Though no longer in use, it is one of five towers remaining in the park.

Preservation efforts are being made by the Appalachina Trail Conference and local residents to save the Mt. Cammerer Fire Tower. It is hoped that it can be restored and used as a museum. Originally, the fire tower had a wooden catwalk all the way around it. The remnants of that can be seen today.

The 5,025 foot Mt. Cammerer is named for Arno B. Cammerer, director of the National Park Service at the creation of the Great Smoky Mountains National Park. Before the peak was named for this Nebraskan, it was called White Rock by Tennesseans and Sharp Rock by North Carolinians.

By whatever name, it's peak offers one of the most outstanding views of the Smokies. A 360 degree horizon allows views of Mt. Sterling, Mt. Guyot, Old Black, Cove Mountain, Cosby, Newport and even the distant Cumberlands. One rainy day we struggled to the top to be rewarded with clear blue skies and a sea of white clouds below. Other times the valley can have a nice day while the top is shrouded with fog. In any weather Mt. Cammerer is a rewarding experience all year. Climbing it takes a full day, but it's certainly worth the effort.

Mt. Cammerer Fire Tower - one of only five remaining in the park.

5. **Albright Grove**
* 7.3 miles roundtrip
* Allow 4 to 5 hours

Elementary children can walk this moderate hike which gains 1,300 ft. in 3 miles and offers virgin timber and spring flowers.

How To Get There: The trailhead is off Highway 321 between Gatlinburg and Cosby. Turn east at traffic light #3 in Gatlinburg onto Highway 321. Go 15.6 miles (3.8 miles west of Cosby) to Laurel Springs Road (next to Jellystone Campground). Follow this gravel road 0.2 miles to a gated jeep road where the Maddron Bald Trail begins. The nearest restrooms are at the Cosby Campground 5 miles away.

Description Of The Hike: The first 2.3 miles of the trail is easy on a jeep road which is also used for horses. The initial 0.7 miles is a gradual climb through poplar and hardwood with rhododendron understory. Several large hemlock can be seen in this section. The old Willis Baxter cabin, built around 1889, stands 0.7 miles from the gate.

From the cabin the climb is a little more difficult. At 1.2 miles the trail intersects the Gabes Mountain and Old Settlers Trails. To the left it's 6.6 miles to Cosby Campground. Greenbrier Cove is 15.9 miles to the right. The trail meanders through second growth poplar at the base of Maddron Bald. Remnants of early settlements can be seen (stone fences and chimneys). A golden poplar canopy covers the reds of maple and dogwood in autumn.

The jeep road ends in a circle at 2.3 miles and becomes a foot trail. The forest takes on a different character with large hemlock towering over thick rhododendron. It's no wonder that early settlers called rhododendron thickets "hells." That's exactly what it is to pass through them. The trail climbs steeply 3 miles to Indian Camp Creek to a beautiful spot to rest or picnic. Enjoy the sound of the water in the cool shade.

The Albright Grove Trail begins at 3.2 miles and is marked with a sign. This trail is 0.7 miles and returns to the Maddron Bald Trail 0.2 miles above the entrance, making the entire loop 0.9 miles long. The bald is to the right, after the junction of the Albright Grove Trail and the Maddron Bald Trail.

This is truly virgin forest containing some of the largest poplar trees in the eastern U.S. It also has many large hemlock and other trees. Take a tape measure to record the circumference of these giants. It's a wonderful example of what the Smokies looked like before they were extensively logged in the beginning of the twentieth century.

This grove of virgin timber which lies between Indian Camp Creek and Dunn Creek was named for Horace M. Albright, the second Director of the National Park Service. Albright was the first Assistant Director of the National Park Service and also served as superintendent of Yellowstone National Park.

The grove is worth the hike. Spring wildflowers are an added attraction to this already beautiful spot. Since fewer people visit this area, the chances of seeing wildlife are better.

Stands of virgin timber in the Great Smoky Mountains National Park contain some of the largest poplar trees in the eastern U.S.

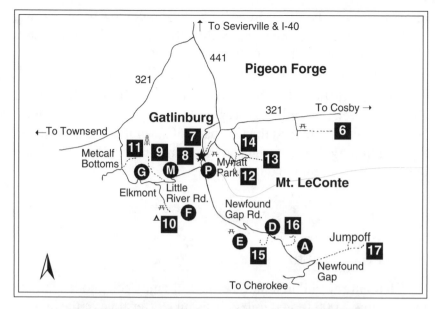

GATLINBURG - MT. LECONTE

Gatlinburg is the northern gateway to the Smokies. It's a popular tourist and honeymoon spot with plenty of shops and attractions. The Gatlinburg Craftsman Loop is east of the town off Highway 321 on the way to Cosby. The Sugarlands Visitor Center is 2 miles from Gatlinburg on Highways 441 and 73. A museum and movie are part of the services available at the center which is next to the park headquarters.

From Interstate 40 take Highway 66 to Sevierville, Pigeon Forge, and Gatlinburg. Highway 73 brings you to Gatlinburg from Cosby or Townsend, while Highway 441 is an alternate way from Knoxville. The bypass from Pigeon Forge to Sugarlands around Gatlinburg, a real time saver during peak tourist season, has scenic overlooks of Gatlinburg and Mt. LeConte.

Mt. LeConte, one of the most popular hiking destinations in the park, is the third highest peak (6,593 ft.) in the park. It boasts excellent views from three of its points: Cliff Top, High Top, and Myrtle Point. The shelter, which sleeps 12, is often full and requires a reservation through the park Backcountry Office. LeConte Lodge, established in 1925, provides food and lodging in a special setting. Advanced reservations can be made by calling (615)429-5704 or by writing LeConte Lodge, 250 Lonesome Valley Rd., Sevierville, TN 37862. Usually reservations have to be made about one year in advance. Sunset from Cliff Top and sunrise from Myrtle Point aren't to be missed.

Since it's difficult for children to make a day hike to the top and back we haven't described access trails all the way to the summit. However, we've included the first parts of several of the trails to the top. Gatlinburg, Mt. LeConte, and the surrounding area offer many opportunities for enjoying the park.

6. Ramsay Cascade
- 8 miles roundtrip
- Allow 5-1/2 to 7 hours

Elementary children and **Teens** will enjoy this moderate hike which gains 2,000 ft. in 4 miles. This hike offers one of the highest waterfall in the park, spring flowers, large trees, and beautiful streams.

How To Get There: From Gatlinburg go east on Highway 321 toward Cosby. Turn at the Greenbrier sign which is 6 miles from traffic light #3 at the intersection of 321 and 441 in Gatlinburg. Follow the Middle Prong of the Little Pigeon River for 3.2 miles. Make a left turn over the wooden bridge. The road dead ends at the trailhead 1.5 miles from the turn. Pit toilets at the picnic areas beside the gravel road from Highway 321 are the closest rest stops.

Description Of The Hike: The first 1.5 miles of the trail is a pleasant walk on a gently graded gravel road with easy access to the Middle Prong of the Little Pigeon River. This part of the trail is suitable for any age and would even be good for a stroller.

After the parking area, the trail turns left and crosses a wooden foot bridge. The trail passes through several large boulder fields which were probably formed 10,000 to 12,000 years ago. The trail crosses Ramsay Branch on a footbridge. At 1.5 miles the old gravel road ends in a loop. The old Greenbrier Pinnacle Trail, to the left, is a non-maintained trail to the former site of a fire tower.

Continue straight ahead on the foot trail which climbs gradually through rhododendron and hemlock. Notice the large hemlocks and poplars. At 2.2 miles the trail descends to a large footlog, then turns left through some large trees. Large silverbell and sweet birch trees are on the left and right sides of the trail respectively. The poplars along this section of the trail are enormous! Try to hold hands and reach around them. The trail levels off for 1/4 mile before climbing again. At 2.7 miles is an easy access to the creek which is a good spot to rest before ascending again.

At 2.9 miles, after another footlog, the trail occasionally climbs rock steps as the cascade is approached. Take extra care when crossing the stream because wet rocks can be slippery and unsteady. Ramsay Cascade isn't a waterfall but a 100 foot high cascade down a rocky wall. It's the highest fall of water in the park and provides the best shows in the wetter seasons of winter and spring. We've seen Ramsay Cascade completely frozen over in mid-February. One hundred feet below the falls is a good place to cross the stream for some good photos of the cascades.

The temptation to climb the rocks and boulders at the base and sides of the cascade is strong. This is **VERY DANGEROUS**. Enjoy the view from the bottom which is a good spot for a picnic. Return to the parking area by the same route.

A good hike anytime of the year, the spring highlights Clinton's lily, silverbell, and rhododendron, to name only a few. Summer is fun because the shady trail offers chances to play in the cool mountain stream. Fall and winter are wonderful times to see the large trees. A light dusting of snow on one winter hike revealed the prints of many different types of animals and birds (but no humans). This trail is rarely crowded.

The Underworld

The Cherokee believed that a duplicate world existed beneath the ground. The only difference between the worlds is that the seasons were opposite. The proof of this was seen in the springs which ran cool in the hot summer months and warm in the freezing winter. Also, caves were warm during the coldest days and cool during the hottest times.

A Cherokee Legend

7. Gatlinburg Trail
- 3.4 miles roundtrip
- Allow 2 hours

Preschool and **elementary** children will like this walk on a graveled pathway beside the Little Pigeon River. It is possible to take strollers on this walk.

How to Get There: This trail can be hiked in either direction, but will be described as hiked from south to north (toward Gatlinburg). The trailhead is at the Great Smoky Mountains Maintenance Center near Sugarlands. From Gatlinburg follow 441 South (into the park) approximately two miles. Turn right on Park Headquarters Road. Continue past Park Headquarters and the road to Cataract Falls for 0.3 miles to the maintenance center where parking is available. A sign marking the trail can be seen from the parking area. The nearest restrooms are in the visitor center or in Gatlinburg.

Description of Hike: This is an easy hike for all ages. Reminders of the past are alongside the trail However, the present interrupts with sounds and sights of traffic on the highway. Much of this trail follows the old road from Gatlinburg to Sugarlands as it parallels the West Prong of the Little Pigeon River.

At the beginning of the walk, look across the large island at the stone wall on the opposite side of the river. Stroll through rhododendrons and hardwoods to where the river reunites in a torrent, smoothing stones and undercutting the ledge on which you are standing.

At 0.5 miles the trail passes under the Gatlinburg Bypass. This stretch is flat and pleasant with cool spots to play in the water. Climb a short incline away from the river to pass between chimneys and foundations of houses from another time. Descend into a flat area where the second growth poplar indicates that this area was probably farmed at one time.

The trail then turns right to cross the river on a steel and wooden bridge. The trail comes close to the busy highway and then recedes into the woods. Allow your children to linger and enjoy the river as you move toward Gatlinburg.

The trail returns, once more, to the highway before it divides into two short legs which terminate at River Road across from Burning Bush Plaza. Return by the same trail.

This trail can be used to walk to the Visitor Center or Cataract Falls from Gatlinburg. Cataract Falls is a nice side trip when walking to or from Gatlinburg. **Take care to hold young children's hands when near the highway.**

8. Cataract Falls
- 0.5 miles roundtrip
- Allow 45 minutes to 1 hour

Preschool children and older adults can make this easy stroll to a nice waterfall.

How to Get There: Begin at the Sugarlands Visitor Center outside Gatlinburg.

Description of Hike: Take the Sugarlands Guided Nature Trail behind the Sugarland Visitor Center. Go on the trail to the right at the first fork. Walk to the Park Headquarters building. After passing in front of Park Headquarters, turn left on the sidewalk at the parking area. Continue 150 yards to the road. Make another left on the road behind Park Headquarters. The trail to Cataract begins on the right after the bridge beyond the employee parking area. It's an easy 225 yards beside Fighting Creek to Cataract Falls.

Cataract Falls is a nice cascade which slides down a rocky sandstone face before Cataract Branch joins Fighting Creek. This is a small falls (about 40 feet tall) which is a nice complement to the Sugarlands Guided Nature Trail and the Sugarlands Visitor Center or the Gatlinburg Trail.

9. Laurel Falls - Cove Mountain Fire Tower

- 2.6 miles roundtrip - Allow 2 hours
- 8 miles roundtrip - Allow 5-5-1/2 hours

Preschoolers could go to Laurel Falls and back. However, **Elementary** children and **Teens** would enjoy the moderate hike to the tower. This trail offers a waterfall, fire tower, wonderful views and virgin forest.

How To Get There: The trailhead is at Fighting Creek Gap along the Little River Road (Highway 73) between Gatlinburg and Townsend. Plenty of parking is available 3.8 miles from Sugarlands Visitor Center and 14 miles from Townsend. The closest restrooms are at Elkmont Campground, 2 miles from Fighting Creek Gap toward Townsend.

Description Of The Hike: The first 1.3 miles is a paved trail to Laurel Falls which is a self-guided nature trail. A leaflet which describes interesting features on the way to Laurel Falls can be obtained for a small charge at the trailhead.

The trail climbs through oak and hemlock with views of Meigs and Blanket Mountains to the southwest. In mid-May the mountain laurel blooms abundantly into a wonderful show of white and pink. This portion of the trail is easy and well suited for any age. Strollers and maybe wheelchairs are able to make it on this paved pathway.

Steep cliffs above and below the trail are reached before the falls, but there's no danger as long as everyone stays on the trail. Hold onto small hands so that no one strays too far. However, at other spots it's safe for children to be the leaders. Laurel Branch tumbles over cliffs of sandstone to form two beautiful falls through which the trail passes. This lovely spot is a popular site. With younger children it's best to turn around at Laurel Falls for a good 2.6 mile hike.

To reach Cove Mountain and the fire tower, cross Laurel Branch on the stones and continue up the trail. The first mile steadily climbs Chinquapin Ridge through pine and laurel mixed with hardwood. One mile above the falls the trail enters a forest of virgin hemlock and poplar. These large trees are magnificent! Children enjoy circling and photographing these old giants.

Talk to your children about how trees grow, adding a tree ring each year. Why did these escape the logger's ax? This stretch is definitely worth the effort from the falls; however, it's more difficult than the paved trail to Laurel Falls. We recommend it for older children and teens.

On top of Chinquapin Ridge the Little Greenbrier Trail goes left 4 miles to Wear Cove Gap. In the spring galax, rhododendron, and mountain laurel bloom beside the trail. Continue ahead 0.9 miles to the fire tower. The first half of the last mile is easy with a slight descent. The last 1/2 mile climbs Cove Mountain. One tenth of a mile from the fire tower the trail comes to an old jeep road running east and west. To the right it's 9 miles to Sugarlands Visitor Center. The fire tower is to the left with a grassy area and large stones at its base.

The fire tower is one of only five still in the park. The fire towers were an important part in protecting the national park and surrounding lands from devastating forest fires but aren't used anymore because it's more economical and accurate to use airplanes. Take care in climbing the tower steps because there are gaps in the railing.

The views from the fire tower are wonderful! To the south is the crest of the Smokies. Mt. LeConte and distant Mt. Cammerer are to the east. Wear Cove, the Bluff Mountain section of the Chilhowee Range, and Knoxville are to the north with Cades Cove and Rich Mountain to the west. Be sure to take binoculars and a camera on this walk. It's an easy return along the same trail. Spring flowers and fall tree colors are attractions on this all day trip.

10. Huskey Branch Falls
- 4 miles roundtrip
- Allow 2-1/2 to 3 hours

Preschool children can enjoy this easy hike beside the Little River to a small cascade.

How to Get There: Go five miles on the Little River Road from Sugarland Visitor Center toward Townsend. Turn into the Elkmont area and pass the campground by turning left. The trailhead for the Elkmont Nature Trail is on the left opposite the campground. Park at the intersection beyond the campground. The road continues past the intersection to Jakes Creek but the walk begins on the road beyond the barrier on the left.

Description of Hike: Walk up the Little River Trail on what was once a railroad bed used by the logging industry in the early years of the twentieth century. The trail parallels the Little River. Benches along the way provide nice opportunities to enjoy the river. Icicles cling to the rocky cliffs on the right of the trail in the cold winter months. Wildflowers abound in the spring and summer. Fall's show of color is particularly pretty in this hardwood forest.

Huskey Branch is a pleasant stream which slides down bare sandstone into the Little River a mile from the trailhead. Rhododendrons crowd around this small cascade. Although it isn't as spectacular as others, it is an easily reached quiet spot where toddlers and even strollers can go.

The name Huskey comes from families that lived in the area. Sam Huskey had a store in the Sugarlands. Huskey Gap and Branch are called after those who lived and hunted this region. The Elkmont area is interesting with its cabins and Wonderland Hotel. Leases were granted to members of the Wonderland Club which was started in the 1920s. After the leases were renewed several times, the National Park Service allowed them to run out at the end of 1992. Much controversy has centered on the fate of the old hotel and cabins. Take a look at them as you enter or leave.

Enjoy this walk in any season. It is a nice complement to the Elkmont Nature Trail or a drive between Gatlinburg and Townsend.

11. Little Greenbrier School & Walker Sisters' House
- 4 miles roundtrip
- Allow 3 to 3-1/2 hours

Preschool children will like this easy hike to an old school and log house which only gains about 360 feet in 2 miles. This hike offers historical structures and streams.

How To Get There: The trailhead is at the Metcalf Bottoms Picnic Area on Highway 73, 10 miles from the Sugarlands Visitor

Center at Gatlinburg and 8 miles from Townsend. Restrooms are at the picnic area and a pit toilet is at the schoolhouse.

Description Of The Hike: Park at the Metcalf Bottoms Picnic Area which is named for the family that once farmed this flat open area. Enjoy a picnic or a splash in the river before crossing the bridge over the Little River. The trail starts to the right on the other side of the river at a gated gravel jeep road. After 50 yards the gravel road turns to the left. Gradually ascend past the water tower, noticing the stones of an old homeplace opposite it. Continue on the gravel road through mountain laurel and hemlock to an old cistern that once provided the water for Metcalf Bottoms.

Bear to the right onto a foot path through pine, hemlock, and rhododendron. Descend to a flat area with mostly second growth forest which was once farmed. The trail follows Little Brier Creek where spring wildflowers abound. Cross a footlog at 0.9 miles and recross the creek on another footlog which is in sight of Little Greenbrier Schoolhouse.

This old log building, built in 1882, was used as a school and Primitive Baptist Church until 1935 when the area became a part of the park. Imagining what school would have been like in those days is easier due to the original furniture and interpretive programs. The cemetery at the church/school has many Walkers and Kings who lived in the Little Greenbrier area. The number of children's graves indicates how hard mountain life must have been.

Continue through the parking lot and up the gravel road. Leave the main road onto another gravel road which turns to the right above the schoolhouse. Go past the gate 0.75 miles to a split in the road. The roadbed with no gravel continues 0.25 miles up to Little Brier Gap with beautiful views of Wears Cove. Turn right on the graveled road to the log house of the Walker Sisters which is 2 miles from Metcalf Bottoms Picnic Area and 1 mile from Little Greenbrier Schoolhouse.

The log house and surrounding buildings were built soon after the Civil War by John and Margaret Walker who had 11 children. Five of their 11 children, all girls, never married and lived in the house. The Walker sisters, Hettie, Margaret Jane, Polly, Louisa Susan, and Martha Ann didn't deed the house over to the national park until 1941, but with the condition that they could live there until their deaths. The last sister, Louisa Susan, died in 1964 at the age of 82.

The sisters welcomed hikers and tourists, allowing them to observe their self-sufficient life style. Let your children roam through the house and over the small farm. Look at the spring house which doubled as refrigerator and water faucet. A corn crib/shed stored the harvest from the cleared land. The spring has a special charm when the sisters' daffodils are in bloom. Return to Metcalf Bottoms by the same route.

Creek play at one of the park's many waterfalls entertains young and old alike.

12. Rainbow Falls
• 5.4 miles roundtrip
• Allow 3-4 hours

Late elementary children and **Teens** will be challenged by this moderate hike to a falls on the side of Mt. LeConte. This hike offers spring flowers, fall colors, a waterfall, and a creek.

How To Get There: In Gatlinburg on Highway 441 turn onto Airport Road at light #8. It's 3.4 miles to the Rainbow Falls/Bullhead parking area. The Noah "Bud" Ogle Nature Trail is on the right at 2.7 miles.

Description Of The Hike: This multiple-use trail goes 2.7 miles to Rainbow Falls on its way to the top of Mt. LeConte (6.6 miles). The trail follows LeConte Creek up to the falls. One is never far from the sound of the mountain stream which falls from high up the slopes of Mt. LeConte toward its union with the Little Pigeon River in Gatlinburg. This creek was once known as Mill Creek because it had 14 tub mills similar to the one at the Noah "Bud" Ogle place.

An overlook with a good view of Sevier County is at a switchback. When the creek comes back into view the first of two footlogs is crossed. Not far from the footlog the creek is crossed at the base of a small waterfall. Many large hemlock with rhododendron thickets border the creek. In the spring, trillium and violets crowd the trail. The second footlog is at the base of the 75 foot falls where the afternoon sun produces a rainbow effect, thus the name.

In the winter, ice from the spray transforms the trail, rocks, and bridge into a beautiful but dangerous sight. It's a nice cool spot in the summer at the top of the climb or as a way station to the top of LeConte. Spring's wildflowers are plentiful while fall shows a wholly different set of colors. Remember that water flow depends on rainfall, so it can be a trickle or a torrent. The top of Mt. LeConte is 3.9 miles beyond Rainbow Falls.

13. **Grotto Falls**
- 3 miles roundtrip
- Allow about 3 hours

This is a good hike for **Preschool** and **Elementary** children which has only a 500 foot rise in elevation in 1.5 miles. The hike offers a beautiful waterfall, spring flowers and fall colors.

How To Get There: From Gatlinburg's main street (Highway 441) turn onto Airport Road at light #8. At 2.6 miles from the light pass the Noah "Bud" Ogle Nature Trail. Beyond the Ogle Place where the road divides, take the right fork which goes through a second growth forest. Look for rock piles left by farmers who cleared the land. At 3.4 miles pass the Rainbow Falls - Bullhead trailheads which lead to Mt. LeConte. At 3.7 miles turn right onto the <u>ONE-WAY</u> Roaring Fork Auto Trail (booklet at the gate). (NOTE: The Roaring Fork Auto Trail is closed in the winter.) Two miles from the gate (5.7 miles from Gatlinburg) the Grotto Falls Trail begins on the right beyond a parking lot. The nearest restrooms are in Gatlinburg, 3-1/2 miles down the one-way Roaring Fork Auto Trail.

Description Of The Hike: This easy trail lends itself to walking side-by-side. It begins in a hemlock forest but gives way to tulip poplar and yellow buckeye. On the climb from the road toward the creeks, more rhododendron are found. An abundance of mountain laurel and fern is also present. Small streams have to be crossed but pose no problem except in the rainy seasons. Trillium, violets, and spring beauty are in abundance in late April and early May.

After reaching the falls, it's fun to walk on the trail behind the waterfall, the easiest way to get to the other side. The pool at the foot of the falls is a favorite spot to cool hot feet. In the spring and fall many salamanders can be found. The falls, which are about 20 feet high, have a pretty good flow even in the drier seasons. Roaring Fork Creek is said to be one of the steepest creeks in the east. It loses one mile in altitude from its source near the top of Mt. LeConte to its mouth in Gatlinburg.

Trillium Gap is 1.5 miles beyond the falls. Bear in mind that the rise to Trillium Gap is twice that from the parking lot to the falls. From the gap, it's an easy walk to Brushy Mountain, a heath bald with beautiful views. It's 3.6 miles from Trillium Gap to the top of Mt. LeConte. The Trillium Gap Trail is the route often used by the llamas which supply LeConte Lodge. The llamas make trips up and back on Monday, Wednesday, and Friday from April to October.

Red squirrel and deer are often seen in this area. Spring, summer, and fall are all wonderful times to visit this easily accessible spot. In the winter, the Roaring Fork Motor Trail is closed. The falls can be reached, but the hike is four miles longer.

Children enjoy this trail because of the opportunity to play in the creek, smell flowers, see wildlife, hunt salamanders, and cool off. The Grotto Falls Trail is a good complement to the Roaring Fork Motor Trail with its scenic views and historic cabins and mills.

14. Baskins Creek Falls
• 3 miles roundtrip
• Allow 4 hours.

Elementary children will like this moderate hike past old house sites to a 35 foot waterfall.

How to Get There: From Gatlinburg's main street (Highway 441) turn onto Airport Road at light #8. At 2.6 miles from the light pass the Noah "Bud" Ogle Nature Trail. Beyond the Ogle Place where the road divides, take the right fork which goes through second growth forest. At 3.4 miles pass the Rainbow Falls - Bullhead trailheads which lead to Mt. LeConte. At 3.7 miles turn right onto the ONE-WAY Roaring Fork Auto Trail (booklet for a small fee at the gate). [NOTE: The Roaring Fork Auto Trail is closed in the winter.] Pass the Grotto Falls parking area at 2 miles (5.7 miles from Gatlinburg) to a parking area 3 miles from the gate (6.7 miles from Gatlinburg). This parking area is on the left before the road crosses Roaring Fork. A sign for a cemetery stands at the edge of the parking lot. The nearest restrooms are in Gatlinburg.

Description of Hike: Walk on the trail to the cemetery which was restored in 1991. Many of the graves are of the Bales and Ogle families. The house across the creek from the parking lot was the Jim Bales place. His family and his brother's lived in the immediate area.

Notice the dates on the markers. One of those buried in the cemetery was supposedly the first child born in what is now Gatlinburg. The tombstones are reminders of previous inhabitants of the region and the difficulty of their lives.

The trail continues past the graveyard over a ridge of pine and mountain laurel. A long descent on the other side follows an old mountain road through a hemlock forest with a thick rhododendron understory. This is particularly beautiful in June when the rhododendron is in bloom. Take care not to miss the trail as it turns left off the old roadbed to cross the creek. After another short ascent, descend to an open area that was a farm.

Explore the old housesite before continuing down to the falls. A sign marks the right turn off the main trail. The house stood to the right of the trail. A stone pile marks the spot of the chimney. Follow Baskins Creek down to a sandstone cliff. The trail descends quickly with switchbacks to the base of the waterfall.

The waters of Falls Branch do a two step off a sandstone ledge to drop 35 feet onto the rocks below. The cliffs show several interesting geological features. To the left of the falls, verticle fractures known as joints can be seen in the Roaring Fork Sandstone. A layering effect can be best seen to the right of the waterfall.

Observe the hemlock to the right of the falls' top. The tree bends out over the cliff. Also to the right, about 100 feet up the ridge is a wet weather falls. We've noticed dirt dauber's nests stuck to the side of the cliff. The mud is from the creek below.

Help children to see that the landscape is being formed and is still in transition. Point out the large boulder at the base of the falls. From where might it have fallen? Perhaps is was pushed out of the cliff at the very spot where the creek now pours.

Baskins Creek gets its name from a man called Bearskin Joe who lived nearby and was known as a great hunter, especially of bear. The creek was called Bearskin Joe's Creek which later became Bearskin Creek. This name was eventually misunderstood and also shortened to Baskins Creek.

Climb the trail back up to the house site and the main trail. A nice side trip which will extend the walk only 0.75 miles is to Baskins

Cemetery and Falls Branch. After returning to the trail junction, turn right. A sign points to the side trail up the ridge to the small Baskins Cemetery. Most of the tombstones have no writing but a few tell of deaths around the turn of the century.

Return to the main trail and continue right just a little farther to observe Falls Branch tripping and trickling off Piney Mountain. The branch isn't wide but makes a long, thin cascade beside the trail for nearly a quarter of a mile.

Another way to make this hike is to begin at the beginning of the Roaring Fork Auto Trail. Park in the parking lot outside the gate. Walk up the road 250 yards. The trailhead which is on the left is not marked with a sign. The trail ascends Piney Mountain for about 0.5 miles. It descends through pine and mountain laurel to an easy ford of Falls Branch. The trail follows Falls Branch as it cascades down the ridge. It passes the side trail to the Baskins Creek Cemetery reaching the junction at the old house site in a little over one mile. This alternate way is the only way to make the hike in the winter since the Roaring Fork Road is closed.

Either route requires an uphill walk to get back to the car. Take your time and enjoy the flowers, the creeks and the history. This is truly an undiscovered treasure in the park. It is not as popular as Rainbow or Grotto Falls but is certainly a beautiful spot.

15. Chimney Tops
- 4 miles roundtrip
- Allow 4 to 5 hours

Older Elementary children and **Teens** will be fascinated by the view from these high peaks at the end of this strenuous hike which gains 1,350 feet in 2 miles. This hike offers scenic views, a creek and spring wildflowers.

How To Get There: Follow Highway 441 7 miles from the Sugarlands Visitor Center at Gatlinburg to a parking area beyond the tunnel. Don't confuse the Chimney Tops Trailhead with the Chimneys Picnic Area (5 miles from the visitor center). The closest restrooms are at the Chimneys Picnic Area (2 miles) and at Newfound

Gap (7 miles beyond the Chimney Tops Trailhead). From Cherokee it is 22 miles from the Oconaluftee Visitor Center along Highway 441 to the trailhead.

Description Of The Hike: Descend from the parking lot to cross the West Prong of the Little Pigeon River on a foot bridge. The large boulders and rocks are part of the Thunderhead Formation of sandstone which was formed over 570 million years ago. A second footbridge crosses Road Prong which flows into the West Prong of the Little Pigeon below the bridge.

The trail divides after the second bridge with the right fork going down to the Chimneys Picnic Area. Take the left fork as it ascends into rhododendron and hemlock. One quarter mile from the parking lot a third footbridge recrosses Road Prong. A gradual climb through an open area of second growth forest, called Beech Flats, has many spring wildflowers, especially spring beauty and fringed phacelia. The creek is crossed one last time at 0.75 miles after which the trail divides again.

The trail to the left is the Road Prong Trail which ascends 3.3 miles along Road Prong to the Appalachian Trail and Clingmans Dome

Hawk's eye views of surrounding peaks reward the hiker who makes the strenuous climb to the Chimney Tops.

Road at Indian Gap. That trail follows what was the only road over the crest of the Smokies until the modern highway was built. Settlers built the road along the route of a Cherokee footpath. Cherokee Confederate troops completed the transmountain road during the Civil War. The Road Prong Trail is a beautiful hike for wildflowers, but is best descended rather than ascended.

The trail to the Chimneys goes to the right. Rest here because the trail becomes very steep. A pretty cascade is half way up the steep part. A switch back signals the end of the steepest section, but the climb continues, though it moderates. Walk the narrow ridge top amid the tenacious grip of thousands of roots. At the end of the hike, the Chimneys rise like a stone wall.

Don't let the last little bit intimidate you. The metamorphic Anakeesta rock formation has many hand and foot holds so that climbing is fairly easy. Keep children close and hold hands! An easier, though not as adventurous or scenic, way to the top is to the right of the cliffs.

The view from the top affords sights of Sugarlands Valley to the northwest, Mt. Mingus to the southeast, and Mt. LeConte to the northeast. Highway 441 and the famous Loop can be seen below. Take plenty of water for this hike. Enjoy the view at the top but be very careful on the rocks. Don't climb in the natural chimney at the top where loose rocks make it dangerous. It's for this hole that the Chimneys were named. Return to the parking lot by the same route.

16. Alum Cave & Arch Rock
- 5 miles roundtrip
- Allow 4 hours

Elementary children and **Teens** will find this moderate hike, which gains about 2,500 feet in 2.5 miles, interesting and challenging. This hike offers scenic views, creeks, spring flowers, and a small cave.

How To Get There: The trailhead is located on Highway 441, 8.6 miles south of Sugarlands Visitor Center and 4.3 miles north of Newfound Gap. Two parking areas at the trailhead are often crowded because this is the shortest (though steepest) route to Mt. LeConte.

The closest restrooms are at the Chimneys Picnic Area (4.3 miles) and at Newfound Gap (4 miles).

Description Of The Hike: Leaflets for the Alum Cave Bluffs Self-Guiding Nature Trail are available at the trailhead. Get a brochure to understand more about the plant and animal life. The first foot bridge crosses Walker Camp Prong and the second crosses Alum Cave Creek. The two flow together below the trailhead to form the Middle Prong of the Little Pigeon River.

The first leg of the hike is beside Alum Cave Creek through rhododendron, northern hardwood, and hemlock. The rhododendron is mainly rosebay which blooms in July with large clusters of white flowers. The creek, which is cool on the hottest summer days, makes a wonderful playground. It's shallow and slow so young children can play safely in its waters.

The trail leaves Alum Cave Creek and follows Styx Branch which is crossed three times on foot logs. Our children enjoy the logs almost as much as the creeks. Holding hands is fun but may not be necessary on the first part of the trail (except on the foot logs). At 1-1/4 miles, cross the creek and go into Arch Rock, a tunnel which was formed by water erosion. The stone steps are steep and can be damp, so walk slowly. A cable offers a good hand hold. Ice can cover the steps in the winter. Several large rocks above Arch Rock provide good resting spots. After Arch Rock, Styx Branch is crossed one last time.

The trail begins to double back as it skirts the foot of Huggins Hell (now you understand why the branch was named Styx). Laurel and rhododendron thickets were called "hells" by the mountaineers because the bushes are so close and entangled it's like hell to walk through them. A thunderstorm in 1993 caused a washout on a tributary of Styx Branch. Trees, shrubs, and soil were washed away.

The trail climbs the ridge through northern spruce-fir which is at its southernmost range in the Smokies. At 2 miles, a small heath bald with excellent views is gained. Look back to see a landslide scar made in 1951. Binoculars or a keen eye may discern a hole in the knife-edged ridge to the west. Falcons have been reintroduced at Peregrine Peak at the end of the ridge.

Relax amid the sand myrtle and catawba rhododendron at the bald. Sand myrtle has a tiny white flower and short green shiny leaves. It grows close to the ground and blooms in late spring. Catawba rhododendron has a pink flower which is usually fading when its lower elevation relation, the rosebay rhododendron, is beginning to bloom. Look west beyond the parking area to the Chimneys and Sugarland Mountain. The Alum Cave Bluffs are less than 1/2 mile from the heath bald. It isn't a cave but rather a large over-hanging bluff about 100 feet high. Notice the difference in the rock from that of the sandstone in the river at the beginning of the hike. The cliffs are part of the Anakeesta formation which is the same metamorphic formation as the Chimney Tops.

A high sulphur content in the rock causes the smell. It's said that this was a source of saltpeter during the Civil War; however, very little was mined because of the region's inaccessibility. Water seeping through the rock and over the cliff's face removes the minerals in the form of alum.

The trail continues 3 more miles to the top of Mt. LeConte. If you're going on, bear in mind that 1,400 ft. of elevation is still to be gained. Allow plenty of time to the top which is the third highest peak in the park at over 6,500 feet.

Return on the same trail. June is one of the best months of the year for this very popular access to Mt. LeConte. Don't let a crowded parking lot discourage you from this trip with its variety of rocks and vegetation.

Ka'lanu, The Raven

As a young man growing up in the frontier town of Maryville, Sam Houston went to live among the Cherokee. He was adopted by Chief Jolly and given the name, Ka'lanu, the Raven. He fought in the Battle of Horseshoe Bend with Andrew Jackson and the Cherokees against the Creek Indians.

Houston was a friend to the Cherokee throughout his political career. He served as a member of the U.S. House of Representatives and Senate, Governor of Tennessee, President of the Republic of Texas and Governor of Texas. He is one of the few men to have served as governor of two states. A schoolhouse in which he taught still stands near Maryville.

17. Charlies Bunion & the Jumpoff
- 10 miles roundtrip
- Allow 6 to 7 hours

Late Elementary children and **Teens** will find this moderate hike a challenge. 1,120 ft. is gained in 3 miles but 600 ft. is lost down to Charlies Bunion. This hike offers magnificent views!

How To Get There: The trailhead is at Newfound Gap off Highway 441, 15 miles from Gatlinburg (30 minutes) and 20 miles from Cherokee (45 minutes). Good restrooms are at Newfound Gap.

Description Of The Hike: Take the Appalachian Trail east from the parking lot at Newfound Gap. This walk is part of the 2,100 mile Appalachian Trail which stretches along the crest of the Appalachian Mountains from Georgia to Maine and is marked with white blazes. The walk to Charlies Bunion is most difficult at the beginning.

The first 2.5 miles is mostly uphill through some virgin forest. The trail is rocky with many roots, so walk carefully and don't rush. Spruce and fir are abundant as the trail straddles the North Carolina-Tennessee line. Our children enjoy standing in both states at the same time. North Carolina is to the south and east while Tennessee is to the north and west.

At 0.5 miles is a good view of the Tennessee Smokies, Mt. LeConte, and the Chimneys. Continue the ascent of Mt. Kephart which is named for famed outdoors writer Horace Kephart, who actively supported the establishment of a national park in the Smokies. Kephart didn't live to see President Franklin D. Roosevelt dedicate the park at Newfound Gap in 1940.

The Sweat Heifer Trail leaves the Appalachian Trail after 1.7 miles and goes 3.7 miles to the right to the Kephart Prong Shelter. The A.T. moderates considerably as it follows the top of a ridge to the summit of Mt. Kephart (6,150 ft.). As blackberry briars crowd the trail along this stretch, look for the slate junco, a small gray bird which flits about mountain summits. We sometimes run across grouse and red squirrel on this particular walk. A grouse will flap its wings against the ground as it takes off, making a BOOM to scare and distract any intruder.

Good views of North Carolina are at the summit of Mt. Kephart. The Boulevard Trail to Mt. LeConte (5.2 miles away) breaks off to the left at 2.6 miles. The Jumpoff is a spectacular view 0.5 mile from this trail junction. (See below.) Take the right fork and descend to the Ice Water Spring Shelter, a stone shelter which sleeps 12. Reservations through the Backcountry Office are required for this often crowded shelter. The last mile to Charlies Bunion is mostly downhill along a rocky trail. Don't drink the water from Ice Water Spring unless it's properly treated. It looks inviting but could cause illness.

Charlies Bunion is a rocky outcrop that was denuded by a forest fire in 1925. Heavy rains and winds scoured this summit which was supposedly named for Charlie Conner by Horace Kephart. The story is that Charlie Conner had a sore foot and removed his boot as they rested on the rocky outcrop in 1929.

The views are spectacular! To the northeast is the Jumpoff and Mt. LeConte with Horseshoe Mountain and Greenbrier Pinnacle to the north. Mt. Guyot, Old Black, and Mt. Chapman are to the northeast. To the south is Richland Mountain, Thomas Divide, and the Qualla Indian Reservation. CAUTION: DON'T CLIMB TOO NEAR THE EDGE!!!

Return to Newfound Gap by the same route. The best time of the year is between late spring and early fall. The trail is icy and dangerous during the winter. It's cool amid the mountain breezes in the summer. Sometimes it snows as late as early May. Don't miss Charlies Bunion, one of the best views in the Smokies!

The Jumpoff

The Boulevard Trail which goes 5.2 miles to Mt. LeConte, leaves the A.T. at 2.7 miles from Newfound Gap. Walk on the Boulevard Trail 100 paces looking carefully for the sign to the Jumpoff. The trail, which angles off to the right, is narrow and slightly rough. For the most part, it's level atop the northern ridge of Mt. Kephart. The Jumpoff is less than 0.5 miles from the sign. Blackberry bushes at the beginning give way to a spruce-fir forest.

The cliffs provide an excellent view to the north and east. Charlies Bunion along the A.T. and Porter's Creek are seen below. Greenbrier

Pinnacle, Old Black, Mt. Guyot, and Mt. Chapman are also sights from this cliff top. Once we started on a pretty fall day only to ascend into clouds. When we arrived at the Jumpoff, it was so foggy that nothing could be seen. An eight year old gasped, "It's the edge of the world!" There was no horizon, no valley, no sky - only gray fog.

Any season is good for the Jumpoff; however, summer has the most haze or "smoke" from which the mountains get their name. Just remember that it's cool on the top of the Smokies. A trip in late May will mean early spring weather. The Jumpoff is an easy side trip which is well worth the time on the way to or from Charlies Bunion, Mt. LeConte, or it can be a great trip in its own right.

A hike to Charlies Bunion is fun in any season.

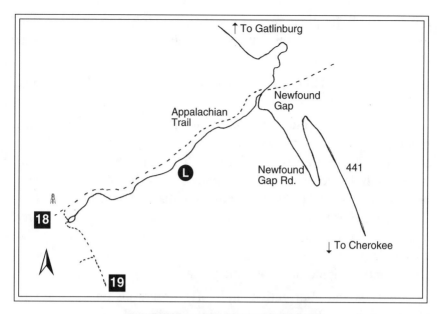

CLINGMANS DOME

Clingmans Dome is the highest peak in the Great Smoky Mountains National Park at 6,641 feet. In spite of its great height, it's the most accessible summit because it's possible to drive nearly to the top. An observation tower at the top affords fantastic views which are available to everyone, even people in strollers and wheelchairs. Turn onto the seven mile Clingmans Dome Road as it leaves Highway 441 at Newfound Gap. This intersection is 27 miles (one hour) from Cherokee and 22 miles (45 min.) from Gatlinburg. The Clingmans Dome Road is closed in the winter (from November to April). Plenty of parking is available at the Forney Ridge Parking Area which has good restrooms. For a limited stay in the park, Clingmans Dome is a must see.

18. Clingmans Dome
- 1 mile roundtrip
- Allow 45 minutes to 1 hour

Preschool and **Elementary** children will enjoy the views from the tower on this easy to moderate hike which gains 330 feet in 0.5

miles. With frequent rest stops it is possible for strollers and wheelchairs to traverse this paved trail. The hike offers fine views and the spruce-fir forest.

How To Get There: The trail begins at the Forney Ridge Parking Area.

Description Of The Hike: The trail is paved all the way to the top, making it good for strollers and wheelchairs. The spruce-fir forest through which the trail ascends is dying due to an infestation of balsam woolly aphids and to acid rain. Studies of the effects of acid rain are being conducted near the summit of Clingmans Dome. Over 95% of the mature Fraser fir trees have been affected by the aphids, a tiny insect. Park resource managers are trying to save some of the surviving trees. The Fraser fir grows only in the Southern Appalachians and is a candidate for listing as an endangered species.

Benches and interpretive signs offer rest stops on the way up. Don't rush in the thinner air of the high Smokies. Enjoy the smell of the spruce-fir forest and the songs of the birds.

The tower at the summit affords great views (360 degrees). Picture maps orient the observer to the surrounding peaks which are magnificent on clear days. Remember, however, that just because it's clear in the valley doesn't mean it's clear at the summit which often will be cloaked in fog. The return to the car is easy.

In the winter, the summit can only be reached along a seven mile walk since the road is closed due to ice and snow. The Appalachian Trail reaches the highest point of its entire 2,100 mile length when it crosses the summit only a few yards from the base of the observation tower.

One experiment we enjoy is to seal a canteen or bottle in Gatlinburg or Cherokee and listen to it pop when it's opened at the summit. This is due to the great change in air pressure. Another way to illustrate this is to partially fill a balloon in the lowlands and watch it fill out as the car climbs.

The drive over Newfound Gap along Highway 441 and along the Clingmans Dome Road are the only places in the park to ride through the northern spruce-fir forests. It's said that driving from Gatlinburg or Cherokee to Newfound Gap is the same climate change as driving from Tennessee to Canada. While at Clingmans Dome, walk to Andrews Bald and the Spruce-Fir Nature Trail.

19. Andrews Bald
- 4.2 miles roundtrip
- Allow 3 to 4 hours

Elementary children will enjoy this moderate hike which is 630 feet below the starting point. This hike offers excellent views, a grassy bald, and spring flowers.

How To Get There: The hike begins at the Forney Ridge Parking Area below Clingmans Dome.

Description Of The Hike: Use the Forney Ridge Trail which begins to the left of the paved trail up Clingmans Dome. The Forney Ridge Trail is a rocky foot trail; therefore, we don't recommend it for preschool children because it's difficult for little feet to negotiate. At 0.1 mile, the trail divides. Take a left at the sign because straight ahead leads to the Appalachian Trail.

For 0.9 miles, the trail descends along the western slope of Forney Ridge which burned in the 1920s. Some spruce-fir is still living in spite of the balsam woolly aphid, but most of the trees are dead or dying.

At 1 mile, the trail surface becomes easier. As it continues along the crest of Forney Ridge, the forest becomes denser. The Forney Creek Trail leaves to the right at 1.1 miles on its way to Fontana Lake 11 miles away. The last mile in the spruce-fir forest is very pleasant with many ferns. From the bald, great views of Fontana Lake and the North Carolina mountains are to the south and east. The Smokies' crest is easily seen to the west.

This large grassy bald has a wonderful show of flame azalea and rhododendron in June. The faint sweet smell of rhododendron and blackberry blossoms hangs in the fresh mountain air. Andres Thompson, a Confederate volunteer who settled in the valley below in the 1850s, grazed his cattle on the bald. The bald was called "Andres' Bald" but a mapmaker wrote it down as Andrews and the name stuck.

The blueberries which ripen in September provide a tasty snack. Our children love this spot because they have the feeling they are on top of the world. They romp, play, and run in the thick grass. Take lunch and allow plenty of time. Ponder the expanse of the mountains and nature itself as your children explore. From spring to late fall, one can hardly go wrong with this hike. Andrews Bald, in combination with Clingmans Dome Tower and the Spruce-Fir Nature Trail, can make a wonderful day to get a sense of the beauty and grandeur of the Great Smoky Mountains. This is the easiest bald for children to reach. If you've only one day and can make only one hike, Andrews Bald may be your best choice.

Relaxing "on top of the world" at Andrews Bald.

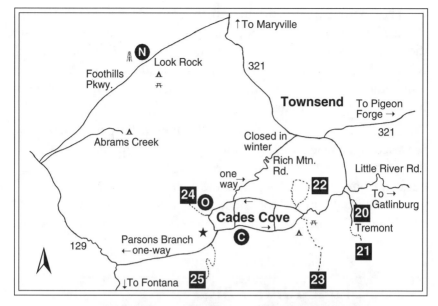

CADES COVE - TOWNSEND

Cades Cove is a picturesque mountain valley in the western part of the park. Its popularity is due to outstanding scenery and plentiful wildlife. The 11 mile loop road is a popular auto trail especially in the fall. The Cades Cove Visitor Center is half way around the one way loop road at Cable Mill. Townsend, once a logging center, is a small town at the entrance of the Great Smoky Mountains National Park nearest Cades Cove.

Highway 321 runs 20 miles from Maryville and 15 miles from Pigeon Forge to Townsend. From Gatlinburg, take Highway 73, 18 miles to the "Y," which is an intersection of roads and rivers that is very popular for picnicking, swimming and tubing. It's only 7 more miles from the "Y" to Cades Cove where there is a campground and picnic area with restrooms and phones.

The Laurel Creek Road is the only way into the cove, but there are two additional ways out, each being one way gravel roads. The Rich Mountain Road goes over Rich Mountain to Townsend, and the Parson's Branch Road traverses Hannah Mountain to Highway 129 at Chilhowee Lake. Both routes are closed in the winter.

The Cherokee had a settlement in the cove which was called "Otter Place". This settlement was occupied even after whites began to settle the area. It's said that the cove was named after a Cherokee "Chief Kade" while others maintain that it was named for Chief Abraham's wife, Kate. In either case, the name was derived from the original inhabitants, the Cherokee.

Cades Cove, one of the most popular areas in the park, can be very crowded. Plan to leave early in the morning to avoid traffic and to see the most wildlife. Deer, bear, turkey, fox, groundhogs, and more can be seen from your car. Bicycling the cove is fun. You don't have to go the entire 11 mile loop since two roads cut across the cove providing short-cuts. Horseback riding is also available. All seasons are beautiful in the cove.

20. Spruce Flats Falls
- 2 miles roundtrip
- Allow 1-1/2 to 2 hours

Elementary children will like the challenge of this moderate hike to a gorgeous set of waterfalls.

How to Get There: From the intersection of Little River Road and Laurel Creek Road, go 0.2 miles toward Cades Cove (west) and turn at the Tremont sign. Follow the Tremont Road 2 miles to the Great Smoky Mountains Institute which is on the left across the Middle Prong of the Little River. Turn left and cross the bridge to park at the Institute parking lot. The office has a sales area with books, posters and resources on the park, as well as restrooms.

Description of Hike: Walk on the road from the parking area to the employee housing beyond the Institute buildings to a path that is marked "Falls." After 30 feet the trail turns left and climbs the side of the ridge through several switchbacks past the water tank for the Institute. Don't get discouraged with the steepness at the beginning. Several signs mark the way. The trail is high above the Middle Prong of the Little River (sometimes more than 300 feet). A couple of wet weather branches that drain the steep slopes of Mill Ridge are crossed.

Don't allow children to get too far ahead or behind. The ridge side is steep. Continue along the trail through mountain laurel and pine to where Spruce Flats Branch joins the Middle Prong of the Little River. The falls that the trail comes to is 60 feet tall and 60 feet wide at the base. The large pool holds the water only temporarily as it pushes on to the Little River.

This falls is actually the fourth in a series of falls that drop nearly 125 feet in a short distance. Some of the upper falls can be seen from a vantage point at the lowest falls. DO NOT ATTEMPT TO CLIMB TO THE OTHER FALLS. Thunderhead Sandstone, which is very resistant to erosion and is streaked with quartz, makes up the cliffs at the falls.

Notice that the rocks on the left side of the falls are more rounded than the jumble of rocks on the slope to the right. The more angular stones were chipped and blasted from the cliffs above to build a logging railroad bed which is about 100 feet above the lowest falls on the side opposite the trail. The smoother stones were worn down by the water.

This area was one of the last logged by the Little River Logging Company. Early efforts by loggers to cut timber near here were thwarted by Will Walker who, in 1859, settled the flat area where the Great Smoky Mountain Institute now stands. Walker didn't sell the timber rights to the area until just before his death in 1920.

The Great Smoky Mountains Institute is an environmental education center run by the Great Smoky Mountains Natural History Association. It has educational opportunities year round for all ages. Inquire at the office or write the Natural History Association for more information. Children have long played and learned in this area since Will Walker raised his family at Spruce Flats. Camp Margaret Townsend, a Girl Scout camp in the 1920s and 1930s, stood on the same site. The Institute now serves children who come with school groups to learn more about the environment and the Great Smoky Mountains.

Return by the same route to your car. The trail is well traveled but rarely crowded. This is an undiscovered jewel in the park. It is a good complement to the Lynn Camp Prong Cascade hike and the Tremont Logging Auto Tour.

21. Lynn Camp Prong
- 1.5 mile roundtrip
- Allow 1-1/2 hours

Preschool and **Elementary** children will enjoy this easy walk which is slightly uphill. This hike offers waterfalls, creeks, and colorful fall leaves.

How To Get There: From the intersection of Highway 73 and Laurel Creek Road, go 0.2 miles toward Cades Cove (west) and turn at the Tremont sign. Follow the Tremont Road 2 miles past the ranger's house to the Great Smoky Mountains Institute. On the right, a booklet for the Tremont Auto Trail can be purchased for a small charge. Follow the gravel road 3 miles until it ends at a turn around. The nearest restrooms are in the Resource Center at the Great Smoky Mountains Institute.

Description Of The Hike: Cross the foot bridge over Lynn Camp Prong to an old railroad bed which goes in two directions. To the right, a Quiet Walkway follows the old bed 1/4 mile to an old bridge abutment. This short walk through hemlock and rhododendron has many opportunities for throwing rocks into pools and listening to the water. Trees across the trail present no problem and can be fun. Our children like to ride the bouncy trunks for a horse ride along the trail.

Back at the trail intersection near the bridge, the left fork follows the creek along the Middle Prong Trail. The trail is a gravel roadbed which is open to horses (watch your step). It's possible to take a stroller along this section. Ferns, doghobble, fire cherry, and rhododendron are mixed with the hardwood forest.

After 1/3 mile, a bench on the left has a good view of a large cascade. Go to the second bench which overlooks the middle of the cascade. An overhanging rock provides a vantage point of the water as it rushes past. Hang on to small hands! We often throw sticks in and watch them float on the swift water. Look for trout in the mountain stream.

Sixty paces beyond the second bench is an 8 foot waterfall. Look for old steel cable which is left from logging days. Below the falls is a wonderful place to cool hot feet.

Another set of cascades is 1/4 mile up the Middle Prong Trail. Two groups of falls form these beautiful cascades. The first set has two falls. The rocks are moss-covered with rhododendron, beech and doghobble on the banks. A bench is near the upper group of falls which is 100 feet upstream from the lower set.

The Middle Prong Trail continues to the Appalachian Trail 7.5 miles away. Older children may want to walk further along the creek while younger ones may be ready to return to the car. Any season is a good choice for this walk. It's shaded with many good spots for creek-play and summer picnics. The hardwood leaves are a good show in the fall. The road to Tremont is closed in the winter.

The name Lynn Camp, perhaps comes from the many Linwood (basswood) trees in the area. Or it may come from the Scotch-Irish who settled the mountains. A lin (or linn) is a small pool in a creek at the base or top of a waterfall. This creek has many a beautiful lin. Enjoy this walk with the Tremont Logging History Auto Trail, on the way to Cades Cove or with the Spruce Flats Falls Trail.

22. Rich Mountain Loop
- 8.7 miles roundtrip
- Allow 5 to 6 hours

Older Elementary children and **Teens** will like this moderate walk which gains 1,740 feet in 4 miles. This hike offers spring wildflowers, fall colors, a historic cabin, and scenic views.

How To Get There: Park at the beginning of the Cades Cove Loop Road. A sign points to the trailhead past the gate on the right. The nearest restrooms are in the picnic area.

Description Of The Hike: This trail, which is also a horse trail, is great for a bird's eye view of Cades Cove. Walk the road bed to a sign at the junction of Crooked Arm Branch and Rich Mountain Loop Trail. This is the beginning and end of the loop trail. Since to the right is the steepest route, we suggest going straight and saving the steep part for the downhill leg.

The John Oliver Cabin is reached at 1.5 miles. Take time to explore this old homesite of one of the families that occupied this mountain cove until the 1930s when the park was created. John Oliver was perhaps one of the first to settle in Cades Cove in 1818. The land wasn't ceded by the Cherokees until 1819, but often whites settled on Indian land. John Oliver's descendants farmed the valley floor for many generations. Let your children tell what life was like when this cabin was built in the 1820s. Assist them with questions like: "How did they cook?" Where did they get their food and clothing?" "Where are the tub and toilet?"

At the John Oliver cabin, the trail turns right to ascend the ridge beside Martha's Branch. The branch was named for one of John and Lucretia Oliver's children. After a few switch backs, there are good views of Cades Cove.

At 3.4 miles, a sign indicates Indian Grave Gap Trail which runs 1 mile to the Rich Mountain Road. One half mile beyond that junction is a fork. To the left is Turkey Pen Ridge Shelter, a lean-to which sleeps eight. Continue to the right on the Rich Mountain Loop to the top which is at 4.5 miles. Remnants of the fire tower base provide a good picnic spot. Excellent views of the surrounding mountains are breathtaking! Gregory Bald (southwest) and Thunderhead are along the (southeast) crest of the Smokies. The Chilhowee Mountain range (north) is across Tuckaleechee Cove.

Descending the mountain, notice the great views of Townsend and Walland to the north (left) and Cades Cove to the south (right). Pass power lines and come to a junction with Schoolhouse Gap Trail. Continue on the Crooked Arm Ridge Trail. Several switchbacks with excellent views of the cove mark the final descent. At the junction, turn left to the road and your car.

This trail is usually abundant with wildlife. We've seen deer, squirrel, chipmunk, and birds. In the fall, the leaf colors and overlooks are exceptional. Spring flowers are abundant, especially near Martha's Branch. Spend the whole day on this trail or combine it with the Cades Cove Loop Auto Trail.

23. Spence Field
- 10 miles roundtrip
- Allow 7 to 8 hours

Late Elementary children and **Teens** will be challenged by this moderate to strenuous walk which gains 3,000 feet in 5 miles. This hike offers a grassy bald, scenic views, and spring flowers.

How To Get There: The trail begins at the upper level of Cades Cove picnic area which is on the left as the Cades Cove area is entered. Restrooms are in the picnic area or at the amphitheater near the campground.

Description Of The Hike: Begin on the Anthony Creek Trail, which is graveled. After 0.5 miles, a road goes off to the right. Continue straight ahead on the horse trail. The Russell Field Trail moves off to the right at 1.5 miles. This trail goes 3.5 miles to the crest of the Smokies at Russell Field which is 2.4 miles from Spence Field via the Appalachian Trail. A good 12.5 mile loop could be made. However, for families, it might be best to limit your sights to Spence Field.

The walk on the Anthony Creek Trail is through large hemlock with patches of rosebay rhododendron. Trillium, mayapple, dwarf iris, foamflower, silverbell, and tulip poplar provide a fine show in April and May. After crossing Anthony Creek at 2 miles, the trail becomes steeper as it ascends Bote Mountain.

The Bote Mountain Trail is reached at 3.5 miles. This trail began in the 1830s as a road over the mountains built by Cherokee labor. The story is that a vote was taken as to which ridge the road should ascend. Bote Mountain won and Defeat Ridge lost. Since there's no "V" in Cherokee, everyone cast their "bote." The road, never completed from the North Carolina side, was used by settlers to herd livestock to the grassy fields and to haul lumber from the forests.

Turn right onto the Bote Mountain Trail which runs 1.5 miles to the crest. In early May, this is a beautiful stretch due to the many spring beauty. When Spence Field is reached, the wide open places are beautiful! On this large grassy area which is 4,890 feet above sea level, the serviceberry trees (locally called sarvis) blossom in May. Fine views of North Carolina and Tennessee please the eye.

The Appalachian Trail crosses Spence Field making good connections with Rocky Top and Thunderhead, which are 1.2 and 1.9 miles to the east and Russell Field, which is 2.4 miles to the west. Just remember that Thunderhead is a 700 foot gain in altitude and will add 4 miles to the hike.

Allow plenty of time to enjoy the views from Spence Field. Also, since Cades Cove has so much wildlife, there's a good chance that you'll spot deer, skunk, squirrel, or even a bear. Please remember - **DON'T FEED THE WILDLIFE!!** It harms the animals and can harm you. The return trip is fairly easy since it's all downhill. You may be surprised at how quickly you get back.

24. Abrams Falls
• 5 miles roundtrip
• Allow 3 hours

Elementary children will enjoy this moderate walk which gains about 400 feet in 2.5 miles. This hike offers a large waterfall, spring flowers, and a good creek.

How To Get There: Take the Cades Cove Loop Road about 5 miles to a right turn after crossing Abrams Creek. Follow the gravel road 0.5 miles to a parking area. The nearest restrooms are at the Cable Mill Visitor Center which is beyond the Abrams Falls road.

Description Of The Hike: Start at the parking area at the junction of Mill and Abrams Creeks. A footbridge crosses Abrams Creek to a trail split. To the right, it's 0.5 miles through bottom land to the Elijah Oliver cabin. This is an excellent walk for preschool and elementary children to see a restored homesite. (See Nature Walks). Straight ahead at the split is the Abrams Creek Trail which goes through a rhododendron tunnel that is especially beautiful in late spring when it's in full bloom.

The trail generally follows the creek until it ascends a pine-covered ridge. Arbutus Branch is crossed before ascending Arbutus Ridge, 200 feet above the creek. At 1 mile, the ridge top is gained; then the trail descends through pines and mountain laurel to a footlog over Stony Branch. A third and final ridge is climbed at 2 miles. Don't give up! You're almost there!! A footlog across Wilson Creek is reached at 2.5 miles.

A short side trail to the left goes to the top of Abrams Falls. Closely supervise children while on the rocks above or below the falls. The last 0.2 miles down to Wilson Creek can be difficult for smaller children; watch them closely.

The 25 foot high Abrams Falls plunges into a large pool with the volume of water of a small river rather than a creek. Eighteen creeks and branches flow into Cades Cove to form Abrams Creek, which is the only water exit from the cove to the Little Tennessee River. Abrams Creek and Falls were probably named for Old Abraham, a Cherokee who lived near the cove in Chilhowee. A Cherokee village, Tsiyahi, Otter Place, was in all likelihood named for the otters which once frolicked in the creek. Attempts are being made to reintroduce the otter to the Great Smoky Mountains.

Return to the parking lot by the same trail. This is a beautiful walk in the spring and summer providing plenty of wildflowers, rhododendron, and mountain laurel, as well as many opportunities for playing in the creek. This hike goes well with a day trip to Cades Cove. Picnic at the falls or at the Cable Mill Visitor Center.

Historic structures abound in the park.

25. Gregory Bald
- 11 miles roundtrip
- Allow 6 to 8 hours

Late elementary children and **Teens** will enjoy this moderate to difficult hike that gains 3,000 feet in 5.5 miles. This hike offers a grassy bald, spring flowers, and scenic views.

How To Get There: The trailhead for Gregory Ridge Trail is at a turnaround at the end of Forge Creek Road. Forge Creek Road branches off the Cades Cove Loop Road at the Cable Mill Parking Area. Follow Forge Creek Road approximately two miles to the intersection with Parsons Branch Road, which is closed due to flood damage. The parking area and turnaround are just past this intersection.

Description Of The Hike: The trail begins along the east bank of Forge Creek. For the first two miles the trail basically follows Forge Creek through a pine and hemlock forest. The first mile has very little elevation gain and is a cool easy stretch where the trail is padded with pine needles. At 0.25 miles from the trailhead, Forge Creek must be crossed by rock hopping. The water is usually shallow and presents no problems to the careful walker. In the second mile the trail begins a moderate climb as it rises away from the sound of Forge Creek down to the left. Large tulip trees are mixed with hemlock and rhododendron.

Just below Campsite #12, which is located two miles from the parking area, you will cross Forge Creek two more times on sturdy footlogs. Campsite #12 is a pleasant open area under the canopy of large trees with several good tent sites. A walk to Campsite #12 and back to the parking area is a nice four mile hike. It is a good overnight hike for children who cannot travel long distances with a backpack.

After passing the campsite, the trail begins a steady climb up Gregory Ridge, leaving Forge Creek behind. The ridge crest is reached 0.6 miles above the campsite in a drier pine-oak forest. The trail follows the ridge, occasionally dipping below the crest on either side. Although the moderate climb is steady, the footing is good, making for an easy walk. Galax lines much of the trail in this section and blooms in mid to late May.

Rich Gap and the trail junction with Gregory Bald Trail are reached at 4.9 miles. At the junction, Gregory Bald Trail goes left for 2 miles to reach the Appalachian Trail at Doe Knob. Your route is to the right where you will climb another 0.6 miles to Gregory Bald (4,950 feet).

This open bald is named for Russell Gregory (1795-1864) who settled in the Cades Cove area in the 1830s. Gregory loved the mountains, especially the balds. He hunted and herded on the bald which bears his name. Gregory built a cylindrical stone house with large openings for windows through which he shot deer and other game on clear moonlit nights. He had eight children, many of whom stayed in the area to raise their families. Confederate camp guards killed Gregory in the winter of 1864. Descendants of his were living in Cades Cove when it became a part of the park in the 1930s.

Gregory Bald has one of the finest displays of flame azaleas in the park. The variety of colors is amazing! The best time for the blooms is around the third week in June. From the large grassy bald, there are good views of Cades Cove to the north and Fontana Lake and the North Carolina mountains to the south. The Appalachian Trail once crossed Gregory Bald but was rerouted after the completion of Fontana Dam in the 1940s.

Numerous blueberry bushes along the fringes of the bald can provide a tasty snack in late summer. The greenish-yellow knots about the size of a child's fist on flame azalea branches are azalea galls which are watery inside and bitter to the taste. They were used as a source for water and as a medicinal herb. Lie in the grass and imagine the sound of cow bells, the lowing of cattle, and the bleeting of sheep which once summered on the cool mountain tops. Eat a picnic, make monsters out of cloud shapes, count sheep, and take a nap.

The Cherokee called Gregory Bald Tsistu'yi, The Rabbit Place. It was believed that a great townhouse was in the bald's grasses where the Great Rabbit, chief of all rabbits, presided. In the old times, it was told, humans could see the Great Rabbit who was larger than a deer. All rabbits were considered the Great Rabbit's subjects. Now people can only see the Great Rabbit's tribe and the grassy area where his townhouse once stood. Look closely in the shade around the fringe, perhaps you will see deer, rabbit or other wildlife.

The origin of the grassy balds isn't fully understood. They were in existence before the Cherokee lived in the region. However, the grazing of cattle, sheep, and hogs expanded the grassy area which the park service maintains so that all might enjoy it as Russell Gregory did over one hundred years ago. Return to the parking area via the same route.

Billy Bartram's Travels

In the beginning days of the Revolutionary War, a young botanist from Philadelphia, William Bartram, set out to explore the wilds of the South. His travels brought him south of the Smokies to the Nantahala Gorge where he met the Cherokee chief, Attakullakulla. Bartram was impressed with the wide diversity of plant life in the southern mountains.

Upon seeing flame azalea in bloom he wrote: "The epithet fiery I annex to this celebrated species of Azalea, as being expressive of the appearance in flower...suddenly opening to the view from dark shades, we are alarmed with the apprehension of the hills being set on fire. This is certainly the most gay and brilliant flowering shrub yet known." Although Bartram never reached what are the present boundaries of the park, he did see the virgin timber, flame azalea, rhododendron and other plants and animals which the Great Smoky Mountains National Park now seeks to preserve.

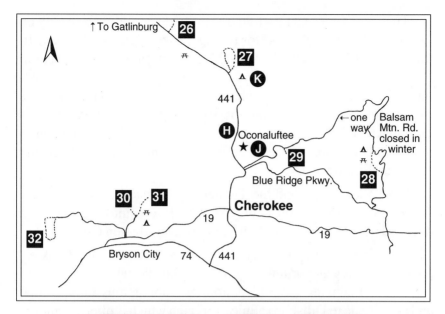

CHEROKEE - DEEP CREEK

Cherokee is on the park's southern boundary at the junction of Highways 441 and 19 about 1-1/2 hours from Gatlinburg. It's in the Qualla Indian Reservation which is the home of the Eastern Band of Cherokees. In Cherokee are several opportunities to know more about the native American inhabitants of the Smokies. The Oconaluftee Indian Village, the Cherokee Museum, and "Unto These Hills," a nightly summer drama, are the best bets to learn about Cherokee life and history.

The Oconaluftee Visitor Center is at the southern entrance to the park on Highway 441 near Cherokee. The Pioneer Homestead is a good interpretation of life in the 1800s, as is nearby Mingus Mill. The southern terminus of the Blue Ridge Parkway is at Cherokee. This national parkway gives access to some of the most beautiful mountain scenery in the eastern United States.

National Park campgrounds near Cherokee are Smokemont (on Highway 441, 3.2 miles north of the visitor center), Balsam Mountain (9 miles off the Blue Ridge Parkway), and Deep Creek (near Bryson City). These three campgrounds usually don't have the crowds of those on the Tennessee side.

The Deep Creek Campground is located north of Bryson City on Deep Creek, which is good for tubing. Take Highway 19 south 10 miles from Cherokee to Bryson City. Turn onto Everett Street in Bryson City. At 0.2 miles, turn right onto Depot Street, then turn left onto Ramseur Street. After another immediate turn to the right, the road becomes curvy. Follow the signs to the Deep Creek Campground which is 4 miles from Bryson City. Tubing is very popular in the Deep Creek area in the summer. The campground and parking areas can be crowded.

Lake View Drive and the Tunnel can be reached by staying on Everett Street in Bryson City. The road goes into the park and deadends at the tunnel about eight miles from Bryson City.

Cherokee and Bryson City are the quieter side of the Smokies, providing many opportunities for fun with the whole family. In addition to the hikes, other diversions are tubing, museums, drama, and a train ride to Dillsboro. Enjoy this area which is often forgotten.

26. Kephart Prong
- 4.2 miles roundtrip
- Allow 3-1/2 to 4 hours

Elementary children will enjoy this moderate walk which gains 800 feet in 2 miles. This hike offers historical sites, a creek, and a shelter for an overnight stay.

How To Get There: The trailhead is 7.1 miles north of the Oconaluftee Visitor Center on Highway 441 (8.8 miles south of Newfound Gap). Park at the pulloff along the Oconaluftee River, 10 minutes from Cherokee and 1 hour from Gatlinburg. The nearest restrooms are at Collins Creek picnic area, 2 miles toward Cherokee, at Smokemont Campground, and Oconaluftee Visitor Center.

Description Of The Hike: This hike is an enjoyable overnight outing with older elementary children who are beginning to have a sense of history. Many elements of the Smokies' history are present along this trail; the Cherokee, lumber company logging, and New Deal conservation. At 2.1 miles is the Kephart Prong Shelter which sleeps 12. Located in a wooded spot with the sound of rushing water to sing a lullaby, this shelter is a nice resting spot. Reservations must be made for the use of the shelter through the park's backcountry office. Kephart Prong and Mt. Kephart are named for Horace Kephart (1862-1931), who's been called "The Dean of American Campers." He was a noted outdoorsman who wrote Camping and Woodcraft and Our Southern Highlanders, both classics in the fields of camping and Appalachian studies. Kephart wrote extensively in support of establishing a national park in the Smokies.

Begin by crossing a bridge over the Oconaluftee River. Oconaluftee is the Cherokee word for "by the river" and was applied to several villages in this valley. A low stone wall on the other side of the river was part of a Civilian Conservation Corps Camp. A stone sign and chimney on the right mark the entrance of the old camp. The boxwoods at the entrance are reminders of the gateway that once stood there. Beyond the CCC camp, when the trail divides, take the left fork across the creek on a footlog. Underfoot are pieces of pavement which remain from an old road.

The forest is mostly hemlock and poplar with rhododendron thickly growing creekside. An old cistern is on the steep hillside to the left. A railroad bed which was first used in 1917 by the Champion Fibre Company to log this area is now the path. Keep an eye out for rails and cable scattered on the trail. At 0.75 miles, the trail recrosses the creek on a footlog.

One quarter mile more, a little detour off the old roadbed goes through some beautiful dwarf iris which bloom in the spring. A third footlog is crossed before rejoining the railroad bed. The trail gets rockier but isn't too difficult. The Kephart Prong Shelter is reached at 2.1 miles. Stay the night on its wooden bunks to listen to Kephart Prong and return the next morning.

This is a good hike to introduce backpacking and the history of the Smokies. It's most enjoyable in the spring when the wildflowers are in bloom or in the fall when the leaves are in brilliant colors. Two trails continue up to the Appalachian Trail from the shelter. The Grassy Branch Trail is 3.7 miles to the A.T., while the Sweat Heifer is 3.6 miles. The elevation gain on each is over 2,000 feet so be prepared for a steep climb! Kephart Prong Trail brings to mind why Horace Kephart worked so diligently to preserve this area.

27. Smokemont Loop
- 3.4 miles roundtrip - Allow 2 hours
- 5.9 miles roundtrip - Allow 5 hours

Preschool children will enjoy the shorter hike which is easy. The longer hike is moderate and will be enjoyed by **Elementary** children. The shorter hike has only a small gain in elevation in 1.7 miles. The longer hike gains 1,200 feet in 2.5 miles. These hikes offer creeks, spring flowers, and fall colors.

How To Get There: The trailhead is located in the upper end of the Smokemont Campground which is 3.2 miles north of the Oconaluftee Visitor Center off Highway 441. Restrooms and an amphitheater are at the campground.

Description Of The Hike: The first leg of the hike is on the Bradley Fork Trail, which is a multiple-use trail. The stream is an enjoyable one in which children can wade and play. It's music is easily heard from the many benches that are along this gentle stretch. A clearing at 0.5 miles provides good views of Mine Ridge to the north and Becks Bald to the northeast. A little after the clearing is an old house site that's easily identified by boxwood that grows to the right of the road.

After the junction with the Chasteen Creek Trail, the trail climbs through hemlock and rhododendron. At 1.7 miles the Smokemont Loop goes to the left while the Bradley Fork Trail continues ahead. Families with younger children may wish to turn around and return by the same route.

Older children will be challenged by the next few miles. The trail crosses two narrow footlogs. The first is long and high above the creek. After the second log, the trail turns to the right and goes one mile up Richland Mountain. Views of Becks Bald to the east combine with many wildflowers such as galax, trailing arbutus, mountain laurel, asters, closed gentian, and ferns of varying sizes to make a scenic walk. In the fall, the leaves are colorful due to many hardwoods.

After crossing the ridge, the Oconaluftee River and Thomas Divide are to the west. At the trail's highest point (3 miles), a large log offers a resting spot before the descent to the parking lot. Numerous downed chestnuts provide an opportunity to talk about the chestnut blight which plagued the area in the early 1900s. Beside the trail are some little brown jug plants. In addition to the unusual brown "flowers" which bloom in May, the leaves are very fragrant. It's said that children once pressed the aromatic leaves in their school books or kept them in their lunch pails.

Less than a mile from the end of the trail is the Bradley Cemetery. It's named for the family for whom the stream at the beginning of the hike was named. Rubbings with paper and charcoal can be made of the tombstones.

The trail descends to the Oconaluftee River. Bradley Fork is recrossed on a concrete bridge, built in the 1920s, above where it flows into the Oconaluftee. The campground is entered on the south end, requiring a walk through it to the starting point.

Plan to play in the creeks. These are good hikes in the spring (wildflowers), fall (leaves and views), or summer (cool creek). The Smokemont Nature Trail is a good addition to a day in the area.

28. Flat Creek
- 4 miles roundtrip - Allow 3 hours
- 2 miles roundtrip - Allow 2 hours

Elementary children will enjoy this moderate hike which loses 600 feet and 400 feet respectively. This hike offers a waterfall, scenic views, spring flowers, and fall colors.

How To Get There: Turn onto the Balsam Mtn. Road off the Blue Ridge Parkway 11 miles from Cherokee. One trailhead is 5 miles on the left, while the other is at the Heintooga Overlook picnic area beyond the Balsam Mountain Campground. Restrooms are at the picnic area and campground.

Description Of The Hike: Begin on a road bed at the Heintooga Overlook picnic area. A water fountain and faucet are at the overlook where views to the north and west reveal the distant peaks of the high Smokies. Veer to the right off the road onto a foot trail.

Grass and ferns grow under the spruce-fir of this northern forest. Occasional flame azalea brighten the trail in June. The trickle of a small creek can be heard after 0.5 miles. The first footlog crosses the upper part of Flat Creek which moves down the gentle slope. Mayapples abound under beech trees along the creek. In mid-June when the rhododendron and mountain laurel are blooming, the fly-poison is also showing. This rarer wildflower is everywhere on this walk.

At 1.5 miles a second footlog is soon followed by a third. The 300 yard side trail turns to the right to descend to the top of the 70+ foot cascade. The creek falls off Balsam Mountain in a 20 foot wide stream. Mountain laurel overhangs the creek above the falls. The Balsam Mountain Road can be seen in the distance.

Pay attention to the sign! **DON'T CLIMB ON THE ROCKS!** It's very dangerous due to wet, slick rocks. Stay to the right of the sign to get to the top of the falls. The small trail to the left of the sign isn't a trail. It's very steep and washed out. We've never been to the bottom of these falls.

The Flat Creek Trail goes 1 mile to the road, but it's a 3.7 mile walk by road to your car. However, you can begin at the road for a shorter walk to the falls. Descend from the Balsam Mountain Road to Bunches Creek and a footlog. A large hollow tree is at the second footlog. The trail climbs for 0.5 miles to the junction with the side trail to the falls.

Either route is good. We enjoy a picnic at Heintooga Overlook or an overnight stay at the campground, the highest in the park at over 1 mile. Late June is beautiful to visit this higher elevation area for its show of rhododendron, mountain laurel, flame azalea, and blackberries. Drive back to Cherokee on the 28 mile one way Heintooga-Round Bottom Road.

Spring, fall, and summer are all wonderful on Balsam Mountain. However, the road is closed in the winter due to snow and ice.

29. Mingo Falls
- 0.5 miles roundtrip
- Allow 1 hour

Preschool and **elementary** children can make this moderate walk to a magnificent waterfall.

How to Get There: Take the Big Cove Road which begins 2.5 miles south of the Oconaluftee Visitor Center. (This turns off of 441 between Cherokee and the Blue Ridge Parkway.) Go on Big Cove Road under the Blue Ridge Parkway 5 miles to the Mingo Falls Campground which is on the right. Cross the bridge to the campground. Parking is available to hikers. Remember this is not in the national park but is on private property. The nearest restrooms are at the Oconaluftee Visitor Center.

Description of Hike: The wide trail begins to the left of the water plant for the campground. The first 200 yards are very steep. Take your time. Even young children can make this if they are encouraged and not rushed. Several benches along the path make the ascent a little more bearable. The trail does level off to follow the creek around the ridge to the base of the falls.

Mingo Falls actually lies outside the boundaries of the park within the Qualla Indian Reservation. The Eastern band of Cherokee have lived in the mountains since the Cherokee Removal in 1838. Many Cherokee hid in the inaccessible reaches of the Smokies to avoid the forcible removal of the native Americans to the land in what is now Oklahoma. This removal was called the Trail of Tears because nearly one fourth of the Cherokee nation died on the journey. The Qualla Indian Reservation was established for those left in the mountainous region.

The water of Mingo Creek drops 180 feet over a bare sandstone face which is along the Greenbrier Fault, one of the major fault lines through the Smokies. Point out the highly stratified rock to children and explain how the sediment of an ancient ocean formed these stones. Stand on the small bridge near the base of the falls for the best views. The return to your car is quick and easy.

A trail goes to the top of the falls but this is not recommended. The path is steep and dangerous. It is best to enjoy the view from the base.

30. Juneywhank Falls
• 1 mile roundtrip
• Allow 1 to 1-1/2 hours

Preschool children can walk this easy trail which gains 200 feet in 0.5 miles. This hike features a waterfall and creek.

How To Get There: The trail begins before the parking area above the Deep Creek Campground, 0.6 miles from the entrance. Restrooms are in the campground.

Description Of The Hike: The trail is an easy stroll through mostly hardwood forest where it's fun to listen to the different birds. A side trail, 0.5 miles from the beginning, leads to a footlog at the falls. The main trail continues on to the top of Juneywhank Falls which can't be missed because they are easily heard. The creek above the falls is a good place to get wet and play.

Down the side trail, the footlog crosses near the bottom of this 20 foot cascade. Stand on the log to experience the water all around you. Extra care should be taken when climbing on the rocks because they are wet and slippery.

Juneywhank is a wonderful short hike which fits in well with an overnight stay at Deep Creek Campground, a hike to Indian Creek Falls, and/or tubing on Deep Creek. A few vendors, located outside the park, will rent equipment. The Deep Creek area is an undiscovered treasure in the Smokies with few people. It's most fun in the summer when the cool creeks and falls are inviting on hot days.

A New Alphabet

Sikwa'yi, Sequoyah, was born in Tuskegee town, near the old Fort Loudon around 1760. With no proper education or familiarity with the English alphabet, he developed a Cherokee syllabary which was quickly adopted by the whole tribe. Within a matter of a few years, many Cherokee could read and write the Cherokee language.

31. Indian Creek Falls
- 2 miles roundtrip
- Allow 2 hours

Preschool children will like this easy hike to beautiful waterfalls.

How To Get There: The trail begins at the parking area above Deep Creek Campground, 0.6 miles from the entrance. Restrooms are in the campground.

Description Of The Hike: Leave the parking lot on this multiple-use trail which is very popular with horseback riders. It's an easy walk beside Deep Creek which is a great place to tube, wade, or swim in the hottest summer months. Children can safely run ahead while remaining in sight. Toms Branch Falls is on the opposite side of Deep Creek 0.25 miles from the parking area. Spring and fall bring out the beauty in this cascade when the water is plentiful and the leaves are few.

The leaves are colorful during autumn in this second growth forest of pine and oak. Spring wildflowers are abundant in this moist clime; fire pink, mountain laurel, rhododendron, and jack-in-the-pulpit to name a few. Take time to play in Deep Creek. Crayfish (crawdads), trout, water spiders, and salamanders are plentiful enough for young eyes to spot quickly. Sometimes it's fun to mark off a small area and see how many life forms can be found.

Deep Creek is crossed on a wide bridge which is a wonderful place to throw rocks and sticks into the swift stream below. At the trail divide (0.9 miles) take the right fork up a jeep road a few hundred yards to the small trail which goes off to the left. Descend to a large pool at the base of 60 foot Indian Creek Falls. June frames the falls in blooming rhododendron.

Take your time on this easy hike and plan to get wet. Wear old tennis shoes so that wading will be safe and fun (but have a dry pair at the car). The walk to Juneywhank Falls is nearby. A ride on the train, tubing the creek, camping in Deep Creek Campground are all great complements to Indian Creek Falls.

32. Goldmine - Tunnel Loop
• 3.3 miles roundtrip
• Allow 3 to 4 hours

Late elementary and **teens** make this moderate hike to old house sites and the shores of Fontana Lake.

How To Get There: The trailhead is at the end of Lake View Drive. To reach Lake View Drive turn off Highway 19 in Bryson City onto Everett Street. Continue on Everett Street until it reaches the National Park boundary. This road in the park is Lake View Drive. The parking area is 8 miles from downtown Bryson City. No restrooms are available near the trailhead. The closest public restrooms are in Bryson City or at Deep Creek Campground.

Description Of The Hike: Begin the walk on the Tunnel Trail which starts at the parking area. Walk up the paved road through the tunnel. This road and tunnel were part of a proposed project to build a road around the north shore of Fontana Lake. The construction was abandoned in the 1960s due to budget problems and the construction of a highway on the south side of the lake. The tunnel remains as a reminder of that failed effort.

On the other side of the tunnel continue on the roadbed. At the end of the roadbed at 0.5 miles notice the terracing work on the right. This was another part of the highway construction. The walk continues on a foot path to a junction with the Lakeshore Trail. For a shorter but less scenic walk back to your car, turn left onto the Lakeshore Trail. It is 2.1 miles back to the parking area on that route.

However, for the Goldmine Loop, stay on the trail which is now the Lakeshore Trail and bear to the right. In 125 yards the Goldmine Loop Trail leaves to the left. Go left at the trail junction sign to steeply descend a ridge. At a saddle in the ridge the trail goes to the right in an easier decline. At the base of the ridge the trail turns to the left around an open area.

This clearing was an old farm site. The remnants of a chimney can be seen to the right of the trail, which skirts the south side of the clearing. Wash tubs, bottles, crockery, cans and other items are scattered about the clearing bearing witness to those who lived and worked here. Notice how the ground looks like it has been plowed. This is the work of wild boar, which literally plow up the ground rooting for food. These nocturnal creatures, which are not natives to the park, were introduced into the area as game animals. Their rooting has created problems throughout the park.

The trail becomes an old roadbed which parallels Goldmine Creek. There is no evidence of gold being found anywhere in the park. The name "Goldmine" may have been a wish more than an actuality. The thick rosebay rhododendron closes over the trail to form a green tunnel which blooms in June and July.

Another house site is on the right across the creek from the trail, 0.25 miles from the first house. Boxwoods and a set of steps mark the entrance to the dwelling that once stood here. Again, many objects from the past are lying about in the grass and undergrowth. The trail leaves the old roadbed for 100 yards but returns to follow it down the creek.

Campsite #67 is 300 yards up a side trail. This campsite is on another old homesite on the banks of Hyatt Branch. The headwaters of Hyatt Branch are on the ridge near the tunnel through which you passed at the beginning of the hike.

Notice the large quartz rock to the left of the trail after the path to Campsite #67. The forest is mainly hemlock with an understory of mountain laurel, rhododendron, and doghobble. Doghobble is the green shrub that crowds the banks of the creek. The waters of Goldmine Branch drown in a finger of Fontana Lake at 1.8 miles.

The trail goes around the shore to the left, crossing a small branch. Ascend the trail as it follows Tunnel Branch away from the lake. The climb is moderately steep through hemlock and rhododendron. Notice the change in the forest as you ascend for the next mile.

Leave Tunnel Branch at a flat area to steeply ascend Tunnel Ridge. Look for holly trees and pipsissewa. The forest becomes a drier pine-oak with mountain laurel in the understory. This is the steepest part of the walk. Take your time with plenty of rest and water when it's needed.

The trail gains the top of the ridge with limited views of the mountains and the lake. An intersection with the Lakeshore Trail is at 2.7 miles. This intersection is where you would have come out if you had taken the shorter loop on the Lakeshore Trail as mentioned above. Bear to the right. It is mostly downhill on a slight incline 0.5 miles to the parking lot.

This area is rarely crowded. It gives children an opportunity to see old housesites and to think about what life and work was like in the mountains before the park. We enjoy this walk for its solitude.

Tsali

During the dark time of history known as the Cherokee Removal, which resulted in the Trail of Tears, the Cherokee were badly mistreated. As one group of Cherokee were being moved, soldiers began prodding women and children with bayonets. Tsali, an older man, couldn't bear to see his family treated in this manner. He, his three sons, his brother and their families attempted an escape. In the resulting scuffle a soldier was killed. Tsali and his small band escaped to the Smokies where they hid in a cave on the headwaters of Deep Creek.

Col. Winfield Scott, who supervised the removal for the military, knew that it would be difficult for his soldiers to go into the mountains to retrieve this band and the many other Cherokee who had fled. He offered a compromise through W.H. Thomas, a friend and confidant of the Cherokee. The Cherokee would be allowed to stay in the mountains until their fate was decided by Congress, if Tsali and his family would surrender to the army.

Tsali, upon hearing the offer, voluntarily went to Col. Scott's headquarters. Tsali and two of his sons were shot. The third son was spared due to his young age. The firing squad was made of Cherokee prisoners who were forced to participate to show their "utter helplessness."

Tsali's sacrifice made it possible for what became the Eastern Band of Cherokee to remain in the mountains.

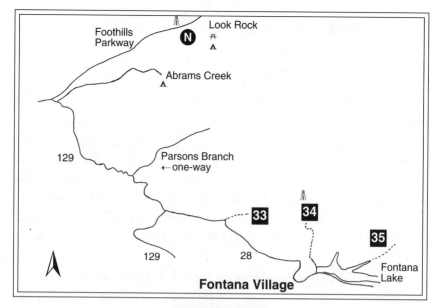

FONTANA

Fontana Village is a resort area that was developed from the housing built for the construction of Fontana Dam. Follow Highway 129 from the Foothills Parkway or Maryville to Highway 28 at Deals Gap; turn onto Highway 28 for the 11 miles to Fontana. Beautiful overlooks are on Highways 129 and 28 which go 24 miles from the intersection of 129 and the Foothills Parkway to Fontana Village. From Cherokee take Highway 19 through Bryson City until it intersects Highway 28 which goes to Fontana.

Fontana Dam, the highest dam in the Tennessee Valley Authority system at 480 feet, was built in the 1940s to supply Oak Ridge with power. The Appalachian Trail passes over the dam on its way into the national park. Fontana is one of the quieter spots in the Smokies, attracting many fishermen to the lake and creeks. Restrooms and a picnic area are at Fontana Dam.

33. Twentymile Creek Cascade
- 1 mile roundtrip
- Allow 1-1/2 hours

Preschool and **elementary** children can make this easy walk to a pretty waterfall amid rhododendron.

How to Get There: Go to the Twentymile Ranger Station which is on North Carolina Highway 28 three miles east of the junction of Highway 129 at Deals Gap and 6.2 miles west of Fontana Dam. The junction of the west end of the Foothills Parkway and Highway 129 is 18.5 miles away. Parking areas are above and below the Ranger Station. The nearest public restrooms are at the store at Deals Gap or in Fontana.

Description of Hike: Begin at the Ranger Station on an old road bed which climbs easily beside Twentymile Creek. The origin of this creek's name is a bit obscure. Some say that it was thought to be twenty miles downstream from the mouth of Hazel Creek. Others said that is drained twenty miles of the mountains. Still others hold that it is twenty miles from the junction of the Little Tennessee River with the Tennessee River.

Twentymile is a secluded spot in the park known to horseriders. The trail is wide and easy to walk. Go 0.4 miles to a trail junction. Twentymile Creek and Moore Springs Branch come together where Wolf Ridge Trail joins the Twentymile Creek Trail. Cross the bridge and bear to the right. It's 100 yards up a slight grade to a small sign marking the side trail down to Twentymile Creek Cascade. The side trail descends a couple of switchbacks.

The sandstone over which the water falls is criss-crossed with streaks of white quartz. The resulting cascades are pleasant. This is a good spot for a picnic or just for a rest on the drive between Maryville and Fontana Village. In the spring wildflowers are plentiful. The return to your car is by the same route.

34. Shuckstack Fire Tower
- 7 miles roundtrip
- Allow 6 hours

Late Elementary and **Teens** will find this strenuous hike a challenge as they climb 2,120 feet in 3.5 miles. This hike features a fire tower, scenic views, and fall colors.

How To Get There: Follow the signs to the Fontana Dam Visitor Center which is 3 miles past Fontana Village. Cross the dam to a parking area that's 0.5 miles past the dam. Restrooms are at the dam visitor center.

Description Of The Hike: Follow the white blazes of the Appalachian Trail up Shuckstack Ridge. A series of switchbacks ascends through second growth forest. The trail moderates after 2 miles. The climb isn't difficult, but is steady. For hikers who are walking the entire length of the Appalachian Trail (usually from south to north), this section is their first taste of the Smokies, which are higher and more rugged than sections to the south.

At 2.5 miles the gap between Shuckstack and Little Shuckstack is reached. Beyond this is an overlook to the south with views of the Snowbird Mountains. The last 0.5 miles climb to the top of Shuckstack Ridge. The fire tower is up a short steep side trail. A chimney and cistern, remnants of the log cabin where the lookout lived, are at the base of the tower.

Climb the tower for one of the best views in the Smokies. Fontana Dam is below with Gregory Bald, Russell and Spence Fields, and Thunderhead to the north. High Rocks is beyond Eagle and Hazel Creeks to the east. To the south are the Yellow Creek and Cheoah Mountains, with the nearby Joyce Kilmer and Slickrock Wilderness Area to the southwest.

The return trip isn't difficult because it's all downhill. A longer hike can be made on the Lost Cove and Lakeshore Trails (about 9 miles to the parking lot). This is difficult and wet (due to many creek fords) and should be done only with teens who are up to a challenge. The Lost Cove Trail turns off the A.T. past the fire tower.

35. Hazel Creek
• 6 to 12 miles roundtrip
• Allow 4 to 7 hours

Elementary children and **Teens** will like this moderate walk which has little gain in elevation. This hike offers wildlife, a creek, and a historic area.

How To Get There: Begin at the Fontana Boat Dock outside of Fontana Village. A boat can be hired for $30 for the first person and $5 for each additional person. The boat can be hired for any day from 8:00 A.M. to 3:30 P.M. all year. An additional charge is made for trips beyond regular hours. To make reservations call (704)498-2211 ext. 277. Restrooms are at the boat dock, and pit toilets are at the first campsite.

Description Of The Hike: Beginning at the lake, the trail is a good jeep road which follows beautiful Hazel Creek all the way up the valley. Three tenths of a mile from the lake is the Proctor campsite (#86). This scenic site has picnic tables and two pit toilets. Beyond the campsite is the first bridge crossing of Hazel Creek. A house and barn which are used by the park service can be seen after the crossing. Continue up the creek through what was once Proctor, a logging community that had over 1,000 people in its heyday. Many remnants of that era remain in the form of large log holding ponds, pump houses and kilns.

Wildlife in the area is abundant. We've seen trees gnawed by beaver, although we've never seen the shy creatures. Deer and raccoon come into campsites to graze or forage. Signs of wild boar (where the ground looks plowed) are along the trail. Fishing for trout is popular on this premium stream.

After two more bridges, the Sawdust Pile Campsite (#85) is 3.3 miles from the lake. This campsite is nice for overnight camping or a picnic. The trail splits after the campsite with a sign warning that the trail to the right is closed due to bridges being out. The bridges have been repaired but are open to foot traffic only. We think the trip to the right (the lower trail) is the more scenic, but we go up one way and return the other. The two come together again a mile ahead.

Two more campsites which are flat and scenic are available at 4.9 and 5.6 miles. The first site is at the junction with Sugar Fork Trail, which goes over Jenkins Ridge to Eagle Creek, while the second site is at the mouth of BoneValley. The walk up Bone Valley, 1.7miles one way, is beautiful but wet due to four creek fords. We enjoy it because it's remote and offers many opportunities to see wildlife.

A long day hike from the lake to Bone Valley is 14.6 miles roundtrip. We enjoy staying overnight at one of the campsites, walking around some, then returning on the next day. This is an easy walk for children to begin backpacking. However, a day hike beyond Proctor to the Saw Dust Pile Campsite is also nice for a total of 6.6 miles.

The boat ride, a roaring creek, and remnants of old buildings combine to make this an interesting and exciting trip for elementary children. We've been serenaded by barred owls and whippoorwills under a starlit sky beside this beautiful mountain stream. May brings the mountain laurel in pink and white profusion, while June has rhododendron blooms. The fall displays many leaf colors. We think this is one of the best bets for camping with children, but it also makes a great day trip.

Nature's many offerings entertain children.

NATURE & HISTORICAL TRAILS

Numerous nature and historical trails wind throughout the park. Brochures, which are available at the trailheads for a small charge, point out interesting features. All of these trails are suited for all ages. We like them because they are good for young children. Most are short and easy with plenty to see. One way we make them more enjoyable is to let the children read the brochure at the appropriate spots along the way. Below is a description of the location and highlights of the trails.

A. **Alum Cave Bluffs** - 5 Miles - Begins on Highway 441, 8.6 miles south of Sugarlands Visitor Center or 4.3 miles north of Newfound Gap. For a detailed description see page 43.

B. **Balsam Mountain** - 1 Mile - Begins at the Balsam Mountain Campground 19 miles from Cherokee (9 miles off the Blue Ridge Parkway). An introduction to life one mile above sea level.

C. **Cades Cove** - 1/2 Mile - Begins 1/2 mile from the Cable Mill Visitor Center on the Cades Cove Loop Road. A good introduction to pioneer life through trees, plants and their uses.

D. **Cosby** - 1 Mile - Begins at the amphitheater at the Cosby Campground which is about 20 miles east of Gatlinburg on Highway 321. 10 footlogs cross a small creek to explore stone fences and old house sites.

E. **Cove Hardwood** - 3/4 Mile - Begins at the entrance to the Chimneys Picnic Area which is 4.5 miles from Sugarlands Visitor Center on Highway 441. A variety of trees and plants can be seen in this accessible and popular area. A good introduction to the forest of the Smokies is provided.

F. **Elkmont** - 3/4 Mile - Begins opposite the Elkmont Campground at a small parking area. An introductory lesson in "reading the landscape" is fun for elementary children who can observe the forest.

G. **Laurel Falls** - 2-1/2 Miles - Begins at Fighting Creek Gap on Little River Road (Highway 73) between Gatlinburg and Townsend. Parking is 3.8 miles from Sugarlands Visitor Center and 14 miles from Townsend. For details of the trail see page 32.

H. **Mingus Mill** - 1/2 Mile - Begins 1/2 mile north of the Oconaluftee Visitor Center off Newfound Gap Road (Highway 441). Restrooms are available at the parking lot. A turbinemill, built in 1886, is in operation on the site of one built in the 1700s. Watch grain being ground to meal and flour at this living history demonstration. Walk beyond the mill, past the flume, to a jeep road which circles back to the parking area.

I. **Noah "Bud" Ogle Place** - 3/4 Mile - Begins on the Cherokee Orchard Road outside of Gatlinburg. Turn off Highway 441 onto Airport Road at traffic light #8 and drive 2.7 miles to a parking area. A log house, barn and tub mill are good introductions to life in the Smokies. One of our favorites!

J. **Mountain Farm Museum** - 1/4 Mile - Located at the Oconaluftee Visitor Center north of Cherokee. This historical demonstration allows your family to participate in the life of a nineteenth century farm.

K. **Smokemont** - 3/4 Mile - Begins in the Smokemont Campground which is off Newfound Gap Road (Highway 441) 3.2 miles north of the Oconaluftee Visitor Center. The diverse vegetation and logging history are explored.

L. **Spruce/Fir** - 1/4 Mile - Begins on the Clingmans Dome Road about 3 miles from Newfound Gap on Hwy. 441. This trail introduces the spruce/fir forest which is not found farther south than the Smokies. Much of the spruce/fir trees are under attack from the balsam woolly adelgid.

M. **Sugarlands** - 1 Mile - Begins behind the Sugarlands Visitor Center which is 2 miles south of Gatlinburg on Newfound Gap Road (Highway 441). The trail includes a log cabin, creek, rhodendron and second growth of forest. A good trail in combination with the exhibits in the visitor center.

N. **Look Rock Tower** - 1/2 Mile - Begins opposite a parking area located about 10 miles from Highway 321 (near Townsend) along the Foothills Parkway and 7 miles from Hwy. 129 at Chilhowee Lake. The observation tower is accessible along a paved path. A ramp goes to the top where the Smokies and the Tennessee Valley are seen. This isn't a self-guided nature trail but has wonderful views.

O. **Elijah Oliver Cabin** - 1 Mile - Begins at the trailhead for Abrams Falls Trail which is located about 5 miles along the Cades Cove Loop Road. The old homestead has a log house, corn crib, smokehouse and spring house. This isn't a self-guided nature trail but is a nice short hike.

P. **Sugarlands All-Access Trail** - 1/2 Mile - A concrete path designed for persons with disabilities. The interpretive signs are in relief and Braille.

CAR TRAVEL & AUTO TOURS

The best way to get a feel for the Smokies is to walk along the trails, to wade the creeks, to peer through the bluish haze at the distant horizon. However, getting to these experiences means a ride in a car. Riding can sometimes be the most difficult part of the trip. We've done many things to make the drive easier and to pass the time. The following are our best suggestions which were born in desperate moments.

1. **The License Plate Game** - This old standby is wonderful in the most visited national park in the U.S. Simply list the states and Canadian provinces you see. One afternoon we saw 35 states!

2. **Looking Contests** - Offer a small prize or reward for the one who sees the first deer, bear, flower, tree, etc. A variation is to keep a total of things observed. This is good in Cades Cove because the wildlife is abundant.

3. **Bingo** - Make up bingo cards with things that will be seen along the way. As the child sees the object she puts an X on the square.

4. **Sing** - You don't have to be an opera or rock star for this to be fun. Standards for this area are: "On Top of Old Smoky," "She'll Be Comin' Round the Mountain," "I've Been Working on the Railroad," "Old McDonald Had a Farm," etc.

5. **Storytelling** - Tell stories from your own childhood, tell stories from the mountains or the Cherokee (See Resource List pg. 68), make up stories as a family. Make up a story using your own children as characters in the Smokies. Another way to make up a story is with a stone which is passed from one person to another. The person with the stone gets to add the next sentence or two to the story.

6. **Read** - Pick out a good book to read a little at a time. Keep your audience hanging. This is a good way to introduce your children to some classics. Read some of the National Park literature, and allow others in the car to take turns reading. On the Guided Auto Tours let the children do the reading.

7. **Listen To Tapes** - Music, stories, books - anything that your children enjoy listening to. We carry a Walkman™ for each child. This allows the child to listen to whatever he wishes.

8. **Games** - Many popular games have car editions. Also card games are fun and easy to play.

9. **Maps** - Older children enjoy reading maps. Give each child her own map. Allow them to navigate by giving directions, or simply let them tell where the car is at the moment.

10. **When All Else Fails** - Simply Stop. Pull off at a scenic overlook, alongside a creek or river, at a Quiet Walkway or almost any place. Get out of the car! Even if the kids don't calm down, you'll feel better and will be more patient.

Nothing works every time. No method is foolproof. Help them enjoy being together with you in the car. Try having a special bag or box of tricks. String them along for as long as you can.

Remember what it was like to travel when you were a child. Your concept of a short ride and your child's are very different. Sit in different seats occasionally. The adults don't always have to sit up front. (Also, parents should take turns driving. This prevents the same parent from always having to be the disciplinarian or the navigator.) Simply put, try not to overdo it. Make the car a place for Time Well Spent.

Self-Guided Auto Tours

Self-guided auto tours are available in the park. These are through scenic areas with historical interest. We've enjoyed all of them because numerous stops provide plenty of occasions to romp, learn and play. Booklets are available at the beginning of each tour for a small charge.

Cades Cove - Seven miles from Townsend, the 11 mile loop shows life in a mountain community with cabins, houses, churches, cemeteries, and a mill. The Cades Cove Visitor Center is half way around the loop at the Cable Mill Area. It's open from mid-April through October. Two roads (Sparks and Hyatt Lanes) allow the one-way loop to be shortened while two other roads (Rich Mountain and Parson Branch) are one way exits. This most popular auto tour can be very crowded at times.

Wildlife in abundance lives in Cades Cove and can easily be seen from the car. Deer, wild turkey, ground hog, fox, and bear are some of the animals in the cove. The best times for animal watching are just after sunrise and before sunset. A campground and picnic area are in Cades Cove providing many services. Horseback riding and bicycling are also available.

Cataloochee - Although the most difficult area to get to, it's worth the time and effort to visit this hidden treasure. Exit I-40 at U.S. 276 (Exit

#20 - Maggie Valley in North Carolina). Turn right on Cove Creek Road after the interstate exit. The paved road ends after 1-1/2 miles but resumes after 7-1/2 miles at the park boundary. The 11 miles from the interstate to Cataloochee is itself a scenic drive. The valley was once a thriving community with over 1,200 people. It now contains several historic buildings, a campground, hiking and horseback riding trails and plenty of wildlife. We've never been to Cataloochee when there were many people, so don't tell anyone about this jewel.

Roaring Fork - This tour starts up Cherokee Orchard Road which is reached by turning off Highway 441 in Gatlinburg at traffic light #8 up Airport Road. Follow this road into the park, past Noah "Bud" Ogle Nature Trail, 3.7 miles to where the auto trail begins on the right. This one way auto trail snakes along the side of Mt. LeConte offering fine views, tub mills, homesteads and decaying chestnuts. The 5-1/2 mile auto trail is paved but narrow and winding, forcing you to take it slow and easy. It's closed in the winter but enjoyable the other seasons.

Tremont Logging History - Turn off Laurel Creek Road beyond its intersection with Highway 73 and go 2 miles up the Tremont Road. After the turn to the Great Smoky Mountains Institute, tour booklets are available in a box on the right. This two-way gravel road which goes 3 miles to a turnaround, parallels and crosses the Middle Prong of the Little River. Fishing, wading, and picnicking are fun on this auto trail which introduces the logging industry. The road is closed in the winter.

In addition to the four guided auto tours, several roads are musts in order to truly see the Smokies. We suggest drives along Little River Road (Highway 73) between Gatlinburg and Townsend, Newfound Gap Road (Highway 441) between Cherokee and Gatlinburg, Clingmans Dome Road (off Highway 441 near Newfound Gap), Balsam Mountain Road off the Blue Ridge Parkway and the Foothills Parkway between Highway 321 at Townsend and Highway 129 at Chilhowee Lake.

Two resources for driving through the Smoky Mountains are:

1. Mountain Roads and Quiet Places by Jerry DeLaughter.

2. A Roadside Guide to the Geology of the Great Smoky Mountains National Park by Harry L. Moore.

Both are available at the park visitor centers.

PICNICKING IN THE SMOKIES

Picnicking in the Smokies is a great experience in and of itself. Many drive into the mountains to share a meal beside a stream or at a mountain vista. The national park maintains numerous picnic areas which have picnic tables, fire grates, and restrooms. Each has its own unique features which enhance a family picnic.

Cataloochee - Although Cataloochee is a bit out of the way, it is a wonderful spot for a picnic. Drive around to see the old buildings, walk up the Caldwell Fork - Boogerman Loop Trails or simply enjoy the day. No matter whether you come from Big Creek through the mountains or over Cataloochee Divide from the I-40 exit at Maggie Valley, it's a pleasant experience.

Big Creek - A small picnic area near the Big Creek Campground is a favorite of fishermen and horse back riders. It is the perfect spot on a trip through the mountains on I-40 or for a walk to Mouse Creek Falls and Midnight Hole.

Welcome Centers on I-40 - The Tennessee and North Carolina Welcome Centers, which are located on I-40 in the midst of the mountains, are good places for a meal, to get information, and to use the restrooms. The North Carolina Welcome Center has a fine view of the Pigeon River as it winds through the mountains.

Cosby - The picnic area is on the left before the campground. Cosby Creek can be heard in the woods below. This spot is rarely crowded. Walk on a guided nature trail or up to historic Mt. Cammerer. The trail to Albright Grove is not too far away.

Greenbrier - The Greenbrier section of the park is off Highway 321 six miles east of Gatlinburg. Picnic tables and a picnic shelter are located near the Middle Prong of the Little Pigeon River. Walk to Ramsay Cascades or simply get away from the crowds to this secluded valley. The road to Greenbrier is closed in the winter.

Mynatt Park - This small Gatlinburg City park is on Airport Road a few blocks from downtown Gatlinburg. It is on what was once a Methodist Church camp. Now picnickers can enjoy a moment beside the waters of LeConte Creek before going up the Cherokee Orchard and its many hikes.

Chimneys - This popular spot is on the Newfound Gap Road five miles above Gatlinburg. Tables are near the rushing Little Pigeon River below the famed Chimney Tops. The Cove Hardwood Nature Trail originates in the picnic area. This is a good resting spot on a trip "over the top" or as a destination in itself. The trailhead to Chimney Tops is 2.5 miles up the Newfound Gap Road.

Elkmont - This picnic area is paired with a popular campground which is open all year round. The picnic area is on the Little River opposite the road. The Elkmont area was once heavily logged and was the site of a colony of vacation cabins and the Wonderland Hotel. The Elkmont Nature Trail and Huskey Branch Falls are nearby.

Metcalf Bottoms - Ten miles from Gatlinburg on the Little River Road, Metcalf Bottoms is located on the banks of the Little River. It is named for the Metcalfs who once lived in this area. Walk up to Little Greenbrier Schoolhouse and the Walker Sister's House or eat here on your way between Gatlinburg and Townsend.

Cades Cove - This popular and often crowded picnic area is on the left as you enter Cades Cove. Come early for a good place at the headwaters of Abrams Creek which flows through Cades Cove. This is a good place for breakfast before you start the loop or hike to Abrams Falls or Gregory Bald.

Look Rock - Look Rock Picnic Area and Campground are on Chilhowee Mountain, 9.5 miles on the Foothills Parkway from

Highway 321. This cooler spot is rarely crowded and is a nice place to rest before walking to magnificent views from Look Rock Tower.

Tables on Highways 129 & 28 - Picnic tables are located by the sides of the winding Highways 129 & 28. These are excellent spots to rest from the twisting journey between Fontana and Maryville. Some have nice views of the Little Tennessee River or sit in pine forests. You may want to take advantage of these on the way to Twentymile Creek or to Fontana.

Fontana Dam - A picnic area is above Fontana Dam, which is the tallest dam in the Tennessee Valley Authority system. Eat here in combination with a walk to Shuckstack Firetower, to Hazel Creek or to the visitor center at the dam.

Collins Creek - Off the Newfound Gap Road, six miles north of Cherokee, this picnic area is filled with the sounds of Collins Creek as it tumbles past on its way to the Oconaluftee River. Named after Robert Collins, who guided Arnold H. Guyot into the mountains in the 1850s on surveying trips, it is near where Collin's home once stood. Collins also was gatekeeper and toll collector for the Oconaluftee Turnpike, which went over the mountains. This picnic area is well located for a meal while visiting Cherokee, Oconaluftee Visitor Center , Mingus Mill or walking on Kephart Prong Trail.

Heintooga Overlook - A picnic area is located at the end of the Balsam Mountain Road which is a spur off the Blue Ridge Parkway above Cherokee. You will eat at 5,535 feet above sea level. Walk to the overlook for views of the Oconaluftee Valley and the high Smokies. Combine this with a walk to Flat Creek Falls or on the Balsam Mountains Nature Trail.

Deep Creek - This picnic area is paired with a nice campground above Bryson City on the banks of Deep Creek. Many go tubing on Deep Creek in the hot summer months. Walk to Juneywhank, Indian Creek and Toms Branch Falls while you're in this scenic place.

Remember that picnics are for humans not the wildlife. Please **DO NOT FEED THE WILDLIFE!** It endangers their lives as well as your safety. Also, leave the picnic area clean with all your trash properly disposed. These picnic spots are some of our favorites. Many other places lend themselves to a nice meal in the mountains.

RESOURCES

Most of the following resources are available at the visitor centers in the Great Smoky Mountains National Park.

National Park Literature and Brochures (Most cost 25¢ to 50¢)

Smokies Guide *The official newspaper of Great Smoky Mountains National Park.*

At Home In the Smokies Handbook 125 *A good look in pictures and text at inhabitants of the mountains and their lifestyle before the park was created.*

Mountain Roads and Quiet Places by Jerry DeLaughter. *A complete guide to the roads of the Great Smoky Mountains National Park. This is the official guide to the roads but it contains much more.*

A Roadside Guide to the Geology of the Great Smoky Mountains National Park by Harry L. Moore. *A great introduction to the geology of the park with five road tours and five hikes.*

Hiking in the Great Smokies by Carson Brewer. *One of the best guides available.*

A Wonderment of Mountains: The Great Smokies by Carson Brewer. *A collection of columns about hiking, history, flora and fauna.*

Just Over the Next Ridge by Carson Brewer. *A traveler's guide to little-known and out-of-the-way places in Southern Appalachia.*

Trails Illustrated Maps. *The most up-to-date maps with notes on the trail and the park.*

In The Spirit of Adventure by D. R. Beeson. *A journal written in 1914 as two men hiked through the Great Smoky Mountains. The book is fully illustrated with the pictures the two men took.*

Waterfalls and Cascades of the Great Smoky Mountains by Hal Hubbs, Charles Maynard and David Morris. *A guide to over 30 waterfalls in Great Smoky Mountains National Park fully illustrated with photographs.*

Great Smoky Mountains Wildflowers by Carlos Campbell, William F. Hutson, & Aaron J. Sharp. U.T. Press. *An easy to carry pictorial guide to many common wildflowers.*

Strangers in High Places by Michael Frome. *A good history of the Great Smoky Mountains.*

<u>Our Southern Highlanders</u> by Horace Kephart. *A classic written in the early 1900's by one who worked to establish the park.*

<u>Exploring the Smokies</u> by Rose Houk. *A beautiful book which offers many suggestions on how best to enjoy the Great Smoky Mountains National Park.*

<u>The Cades Cove Story</u> by Randolph Shields. *A short history of the white settlement in Cades Cove.*

<u>Cades Cove: The Life and Death of a Southern Appalachian Community</u> by Durwood Dunn. *An extensive study of the Cades Cove Community.*

<u>The Cherokees</u> by Grace Steele Woodward. *A good history of the Cherokee.*

<u>The Trail of Tears</u> by John Ehle. *A well written account of the removal.*

Great Smoky Mountain Natural History Association Guidebooks: Trees, Historic Structures, Birds, and Trails.

Fiction

<u>The Tall Woman</u> & <u>The Tall Family</u> by Wilma Dykeman. *Two good stories by an author from the area.*

<u>Creek Mary's Blood</u> by Dee Brown. *A narrative of Indian life before, during and after the removal.*

<u>Walk In My Soul</u> by Lucia St. Clair Robson. *The story of Sam Houston and Tiana Rogers.*

<u>The Cherokee Crown of Tannassy</u> by William O. Steele. *An early history of the Cherokee. (Ages 10-12)*

<u>The RedWind</u> by Sarah M. Traylor. *The story of Fort Loudon and John Stuart. (Ages 10-12)*

<u>Sequoyah: Cherokee Hero</u> by Joanne Oppenheim. *A biography of the inventor of the Cherokee alphabet. (Ages 7-10)*

<u>When I Was Young In The Mountains</u> by Cynthia Rylant. *A beautifully illustrated book about life in the mountains years ago. A good book to read to young children.*

HIKE INDEX

Attribute columns keyed to hikes 1–14 (see legend below).

Attribute	1	2	3	4	5	6	7	8	9	10	11	12	13	14
Winter						•	•						•	Cl.
Fall			•	•	•	•			•		•		•	
Summer	•	•	•			•	•			•	•	•		•
Spring	•	•		•	•	•	•	•	•	•	•	•	•	•
Grassy Bald														
Tower				•					•					
Creeks	•		•			•	•		•	•	•	•	•	
Historic Bldg. or Sites		•	•			•					•			•
Virgin Forest		•			•	•			•					
Scenic Views				•					•					
Waterfall	•		•			•		•	•	•		•	•	•
Teen/Strenuous		•		•		•			•			•		
Elementary/Moderate	•	•	•		•	•	•		•			•	•	•
Preschool/Easy			•					•	•	•			•	
Hours	6	5	2½	7	5	7	2	1	5 & 2	3½	3½	4	3	4
Miles	4	7.4	4.2	10.4	7.3	8	3.4	0.5	8 & 2.6	4	4	5.4	3	3

BIG CREEK - CATALOOCHEE
1. Midnight Hole & Mouse Creek Falls
2. Caldwell Fork & Boogerman Loop

COSBY
3. Hen Wallow Falls
4. Mount Cammerer
5. Albright Grove

GATLINBURG - MT. LECONTE
6. Ramsay Cascade
7. Gatlinburg Trail
8. Cataract Falls
9. Laurel Falls - Cove Mountain Fire Tower
10. Huskey Branch Falls
11. Little Greenbrier School & Walker Sisters' House
12. Rainbow Falls
13. Grotto Falls
14. Baskins Creek Falls

	Miles	Hours
16. Alum Cave and Arch Rock	5	4
17. Charlies Bunion and the Jumpoff	10	7

CLINGMANS DOME

	Miles	Hours
18. Clingmans Dome Tower	1	1
19. Andrews Bald	4.2	4

CADES COVE - TOWNSEND

	Miles	Hours
20. Spruce Flats Falls	2	2
21. Lynn Camp Prong	1.5	1½
22. Rich Mountain Loop	8.7	6
23. Spence Field	10	8
24. Abrams Falls	5	3
25. Gregory Bald	11	6-8

CHEROKEE - DEEP CREEK

	Miles	Hours
26. Kephart Prong	4.2	4
27. Smokemont Loop	3.4	2
Smokemont Loop	5.9	5
28. Flat Creek Falls	4 & 2	3 & 2
29. Mingo Falls	0.5	1
30. Juneywhank Falls	1	1½
31. Indian Creek Falls	2	2
32. Goldmine - Tunnel Loop	3.3	4

FONTANA

	Miles	Hours
33. Twentymile Creek Cascade	1	1½
34. Shuckstack Fire Tower	7	6
35. Hazel Creek	6 & 12	4 & 7

Don't forget to pack the essentials!

MILEAGE CHART

Gatlinburg							
34	Cherokee						
22	54	Townsend					
20	54	42	Cosby (campground)				
41	74	20	60	Maryville			
25	56	9	45	29	Cades Cove		
64	44	42	84	64	51	Fontana	
8	42	15	28	35	24	57	Pigeon Forge

By the Same Authors...

Waterfalls & Cascades
Of The Great Smoky Mountains

"The Smokies were and are carved by water. Water has shaped the mountains and valleys into their present form. Stand on a peak to look down on the jumble of mountains, ridges, valleys and ravines. Look carefully. Notice the slopes, the peaks, the twinkle of sunlight on water. Water sculpted this marvelous landscape."

"At waterfalls this creative action is most dramatic. A torrent pours over a cliff or bare rock face to plunge into a deep pool. Large logs against the escarpment, smooth boulders and pebbles are evidence of the power of water to move, to shape, to carve the terrain."

Waterfalls and Cascades is a guidebook to over thirty waterfalls and cascades in the Great Smoky Mountains National Park. Twenty-eight color and black and white photographs illustrate this volume which locates the falls with maps and text. History, both natural and human, is revealed through the writing of Hal Hubbs, Charles Maynard, and David Morris. Enjoy the magic of the mountains as it is experienced at waterfalls with this book.

"This book is a real prize to those who like to explore all the waterfalls of a given area. With the wealth of treasures that the Great Smoky Mountains National Park has to offer, this book can keep you busy for weeks." - Benton MacKaye Trail Association Newsletter

"As one who considers himself pretty well up on the trails and waterfalls of the Smokies, I was blown away by the number of falls I'd never heard of. This is a must-have book for the outdoor - particularly the Smokies - enthusiast." - Cherokee Hiking Club Newsletter